Helder Pires Ferreira

Customer satisfaction

Helder Pires Ferreira

Customer satisfaction

Critical Success Factors for Marketing Strategies

ScienciaScripts

Imprint
Any brand names and product names mentioned in this book are subject to trademark, brand or patent protection and are trademarks or registered trademarks of their respective holders. The use of brand names, product names, common names, trade names, product descriptions etc. even without a particular marking in this work is in no way to be construed to mean that such names may be regarded as unrestricted in respect of trademark and brand protection legislation and could thus be used by anyone.

Cover image: www.ingimage.com

This book is a translation from the original published under ISBN 978-620-2-19507-2.

Publisher:
Sciencia Scripts
is a trademark of
Dodo Books Indian Ocean Ltd. and OmniScriptum S.R.L publishing group

120 High Road, East Finchley, London, N2 9ED, United Kingdom
Str. Armeneasca 28/1, office 1, Chisinau MD-2012, Republic of Moldova, Europe
Printed at: see last page
ISBN: 978-620-7-29791-7

GENERAL TABLE OF CONTENTS

SUMMARY

The aim of this research paper is to analyze the Importance *versus* Satisfaction applied in a case study in order to identify key factors in the implementation of marketing strategies. The object of study was a sample of 225 customers of the company *Futurlab* - Material de Laboratório Lda, based in Lisbon.

The aim of this analysis is for *Futurlab*'s managers to evaluate and identify the greatest advantages and weaknesses of the key success factors.

The Importance *vs.* Satisfaction Analysis makes it possible to identify the most important attributes for the consumer, with the greatest impact on consumer satisfaction and, at the same time, the low performance attributes that need to be improved immediately. In this study and in order to respond to the main objective of the study, the Importance-Performance/Satisfaction Matrix developed by Martilla and James (1977) and adapted by Matzler, Sauerwein and Heischmidt (2003) was used. A questionnaire survey (Wu, Tang & Shyu, 2009) was used to collect data. It was randomly applied to 225 customers of the company under study, assuming a sampling error of 5.8% and a significance level of 5%.

Through the results obtained and an exploratory factor analysis, it can be concluded that the Critical Success Factors identified for the Futurlab company were Pricing Strategy and Free Services, Loyalty, Image, Supply and Stock, Information, Logistics and Virtual Channels. Since the factors Logistics, Supply and Stock and Pricing Strategy and Free Services were positioned in quadrant B, they were highly important and satisfactory in the perception of Futurlab's customers, so they are factors that represent opportunities to gain or maintain competitive advantages in the market where Futurlab operates and it should continue this good work.

Finally, this study not only provides a specific analysis, but also summarizes the company's strategies from a more practical point of view, since the analysis was carried out in a real context.

Keywords: Importance-Satisfaction; Critical Success Factors; Satisfaction; Multivariate Analysis.

To my father...

ACKNOWLEDGMENTS

During the long period in which this work was carried out, several people encouraged me in one way or another not to give up, and I would like to thank them and acknowledge them.

First of all, I would like to thank my advisor, Professor Paula Odete Fernandes, for her excellent guidance, unconditional availability and support even in times of difficulty and discouragement, for her critical suggestions, for the bibliography provided and for the constant revisions of this work.

To the management of *Futurlab* - Material de Laboratório Lda. for allowing the surveys to be carried out with their customers, knowing the risk and challenge this could cause them.

To the clients who took part in this study, for their availability and cooperation, without whom it would not have been possible to carry out this work.

To my family, who never let me give up, who supported me, helped me and believed in my abilities, for their patience and understanding throughout this time of work.

To the friends who have always been by my side.

To each and every one of you, thank you very much.

INTRODUCTION

Marketing has increasingly adopted aggressive communication strategies such as promotional campaigns to stimulate demand. Promotional campaigns include an extensive range of payment plans, discounts, home delivery services and other promotions to attract more consumers, such as a very low-interest loan service and installment plans, etc.

This has led to increasingly demanding consumers. However, there has been an evolution in the way the market organizes itself to present goods and services. This means that companies providing goods and services need to have more thought-out and targeted marketing strategies, which is the best way for companies to communicate with each other.

In the case of a company that sells products or goods and provides services, it is advisable to bear in mind the competition and competitiveness of its surroundings. Consumers are becoming increasingly informed about the products they want to buy. To this end, it is important for companies to provide their customers with the correct information about their products/services, since they are increasingly informed at a competitive level. It is therefore necessary to know the information that will enable us to meet the consumer's real needs, as well as the best way of satisfying and retaining their loyalty.

The aim of this study is to understand how customers can be made loyal, to what extent they are satisfied with *Futurlab* - Material de Laboratório Lda. (hereinafter Futurlab), and to enable administrators/managers to evaluate and identify the greatest advantages and weaknesses of the company's current key factors and possibly suggest changes to some of them so that the company can sustain and maintain the success it has achieved in the market.

This study not only provides a specific analysis of the case under study but also summarizes the company's strategies from a more practical point of view, i.e. in a real context.

Following this line of reasoning, we intend to apply an evaluation tool to measure the degree of satisfaction and importance of key factors in the implementation of marketing strategies and, if the results are consistent, extrapolate them to the Portuguese universe of companies dedicated to the commercialization/provision of laboratory equipment services.

To this end, the study focused on Futurlab's customers. The universe consisted of a total of 1,055 clients, distributed among various types of companies and/or sectors of activity.

The data collected refers to the 2010/2012 timeframe.

The methodology used was descriptive and quantitative. A validated questionnaire survey was used to obtain general information about customers, identify the importance attributed and the degree of satisfaction with each item evaluated by the company under study and analyze the dimensions (Critical Success Factors) of the quality of the services provided. Subsequently, the results of the survey were placed on the Importance-Satisfaction Matrix, adapted by Matzler, Sauerwein and Heischmidt (2003), in order to see how customers perceived the different policies adopted by the company.

This work is structured in three sections. It begins with a brief introduction in which the framework of the study is presented, the objectives are defined, the object of study, the methodology used and the structure of the dissertation. Subsequently, the first point deals with a brief theoretical review of customer satisfaction and the importance of critical success factors, which presents the concept of Critical Success Factors (CSFs), evaluation of the quality of services provided, customer satisfaction as an indicator of the quality of services provided, the relationship between satisfaction and importance and finally satisfaction with service providers/suppliers. The second section presents the research methodology, referring to the research objectives and hypotheses, the data collection instrument, the characterization of the population, the definition of the sample and the data processing technique. The third point is the core of the dissertation, where the aim is to identify the critical success factors in developing strategies to maximize customer satisfaction through descriptive and inferential analysis, the importance/satisfaction matrix, exploratory factor analysis, cluster analysis and the main conclusions of the study. Some recommendations are made and lines of future research on the subject are suggested.

1. CUSTOMER SATISFACTION AND THE IMPORTANCE OF CRITICAL SUCCESS FACTORS

1.1 - CONCEPT OF CRITICAL SUCCESS FACTORS

In order to keep up with technological, scientific and economic developments, today's companies are increasingly required to look for strategies that will keep them in the competitive market of economic society, namely by defining and implementing promotional campaigns to stimulate demand, which include offering payment plans, discounts, home delivery services and other promotions to attract more consumers, such as offering loan services with very low interest rates and installment payment plans, among other benefits that can somehow please customers and, at the same time, not harm the company.

Taking this line of action into account, companies must identify a limited number of areas of activity where the results are satisfactory, which will ensure a competitively successful performance for the organization, which, according to Rockart (1979), defines Critical Success Factors (CSFs) as clear indicators that can guide the direction of the business towards success.

In this sense, and according to Freire (2008), companies should define these critical success factors, taking into account their objectives, clearly analyzing the strategies for achieving them, so as to avoid results that are lower than stipulated, but which allow them, if this is the case, reformulate or take different paths towards the successful practical implementation of these strategies, always on the premise that failure to achieve them could give the market the impression that the company's efforts are less than expected, which would be detrimental to its continuity in the current economic climate.

In fact, as defined by Quintella, Rocha and Alves (2005), identifying and analyzing the KSFs enables managers to gather the information they need to make better decisions, taking into account an increasingly demanding market in terms of innovation and quality, defining possible ways of acting so that the company's development is always geared towards achieving its objectives.

From this perspective and following the line of thought of Caralli (2004), any activity or initiative that the organization undertakes in the areas defined by the KSFs must perform well, otherwise it will fail to achieve its objectives.

Rockart (1979) said that the analysis of the KSFs is an empirical method based on interviews that allows management priorities to be identified, and the results of these interviews are then analyzed by managers for use in the planning and construction of information systems.

The concept of FCS, even if implicitly, has been used by most managers because of the importance of its analysis in achieving the organization's objectives, but let's see how various authors have defined this concept over time:

Hofer and Schendel (1978) defined KSFs as variables that will influence the decision and position of each company in a given sector. These factors will vary from sector to sector. But in a specific sector, the KSFs will derive from two types of variables: the economic and technological characteristics of the sector and the competitive weapons on which different companies in the same sector have defined their strategies.

Boynton and Zmud (1984) stated that the KSFs were the elements that had to perform well in order to ensure the success of an organization, the competencies where constant and special attention had to be paid in order to obtain high levels of performance.

Leidecker and Bruno (1984) considered KSFs to be characteristics, conditions or variables that could have a significant impact on the success of a company in a given sector if they were correctly followed, maintained and created;

Bouquin (1986) defined KSFs as everything the company would do to achieve its long-term objectives, to resist the forces of the sector in which it operates, which is also in line with Porter's definition of the five forces. From this perspective, the company maintains its competitiveness in the sector in which it operates, minimizing competition or, if necessary, envisaging a possible change of sector, with the KSFs being considered, in this context, as barriers that give the company a competitive advantage or a high level of performance which, while not giving a distinct advantage, allow the company to propose a more generic offer of results in line with its objectives. However, a decrease in the level of performance or a deterioration in the maintenance of these factors can jeopardize the company's position in the market or even lead to its disappearance.

Koenig (1990) advocated that KSFs were the building blocks of success in an industry during a certain period of its history.

Atamer and Calori (1993) identified the KSFs as elements that have value for customers and suppliers, which create an advantage in a given branch or sector, from the design and/or production to the distribution of the product or service, enabling the creation of competitive advantages.

Garrette (1993) listed the KSFs as the elements on which competition is primarily based, and as the necessary competencies whose control will enable a high level of performance to be achieved.

Although critical success factors are a very recent concept in business, they were already used in wartime, as Forster and Rockart (1989) quote when they describe Baron Von Clausewitz's strategic method, called 'Concentration of forces', in which a good general was considered to be one who concentrated his forces on the small battles that had to be won, thus guaranteeing victory, as opposed to the 'bad generals' who scattered their forces across the battlefield, weakening their resistance. The same authors also quote Aristotle when he addressed the idea of successful management as that which allows the manager to create simple, unambitious goals, but with objectives that are achievable and measurable.

Even Drucker (1967), back in the 1970s, in his book *The Effective Executive,* said that successful executives spent most of their time and energy on a small number of critical problems or opportunities.

Still in the same context, Rockart (1979) considered that the KSFs could vary according to the organization's changing environment or the problems or opportunities of each manager, since they differed from manager to manager according to their position in the organization's hierarchy.

Baxter (1983) also described that the method of analyzing the KSFs brought up a new series of questions for many managers, since it was initially used as part of a larger plan for developing information and control of factory systems, but later came to be used as an individual method, since it was easily understood, quickly implemented and focused on the manager and his task. The same author also said that this method allowed managers to constantly question themselves about the company's objectives, promoted communication between the various employees, both subordinate and superior to the manager, and was positive for resolving organizational conflicts.

Baxter (1983) also described the analysis of the KSFs as a method that includes two interviews with each manager, a joint meeting with all the managers and a structured hierarchical analysis that allows internal management problems to be solved, with the factors pointed out by factory managers as the most frequent being excellent relations with suppliers, the productive use of capital and equipment and the effective use of human resources.

Of the various authors identified, Boynton and Zmud (1984) give the example of two studies carried out in two different organizations, a financial services company and a public university, which used the analysis and identification of the KSFs for strategic business planning.

In the results of both studies, it was found that the use of this method made it possible to identify its advantages - it promoted effective support for planning processes, it made it possible to transform mere assumptions into valid information that could have an impact on the competitive position of organizations, the concept of the KSFs was considered reliable and enthusiastically received by senior managers and it also served as a basis for structured, high-level process analysis; and disadvantages - the further away managers were from senior positions within the organization, the more difficult it became for them to identify significant organizational KSFs, managers who were not involved in strategic and tactical planning showed difficulty in dealing with the conceptual nature of KSFs, and it was difficult for some of the managers to define their needs using this analysis alone.

In the same vein, Bailey (1987) described a study carried out in an American private company, where the aim was to advise the management department on how to draw up a strategic action plan that would unite the different types of managers in a common objective. In this study, the KSF analysis method was applied and the results showed that this method was considered to be a valid tool for developing strategic action plans, since it promoted strategic reflection by managers beyond what was initially envisaged, as well as allowing the company to conclude on the need to review the KSFs every six months, or even extend this type of analysis to higher levels of the organization's hierarchy. With the positive results achieved, the company considered the analysis of the KSFs to be an extremely important method for defining action plans, tracking their progress and retaining the managers who had invested in implementing solutions.

According to the various definitions found, it can be seen that the KSFs cannot be defined in a watertight way. On the contrary, and in line with what Quintella, Rocha and Alves (2005) state, the KSFs are not a standardized set of measures which are often called 'key indicators', On the contrary, the KSFs are elements of great importance for a manager in a particular sector of the organization over a given period of time, as they enable the successful achievement or otherwise of the objectives defined for its maintenance in the market.

In order to have a common thread in the definition of the KSFs, Porter, quoted by Quintella, Rocha and Alves (2005), identified the Rockart method as a strategy which, using the various characteristics and contexts of the organization and the prognoses, allowed a set of KSFs to be deduced beforehand and subsequently validated, validate them empirically, through interviews and/or questionnaires, always safeguarding the temporal limitation of these factors which may have been deduced for various reasons, namely economic, political, social or competitive changes, or even as a strategy for change in the organization itself.

A clear example of this time limitation is described by Wu, Tang and Shyu (2009), whose study in Taiwan identified a change in consumption patterns, a reduction in the life cycle of products, and marketing channels becoming more popular. At the same time, companies faced internal limitations such as a shortage of resources, insufficient market information and limitations in the development of technologies, which led company managers to identify critical success factors in order to organize their resources and integrate technologies effectively in order to generate profits and sustained development.

In this context, Waal and Gerritsen-Medema (2006) also considered that the critical success factors would allow management to develop and execute policies effectively and efficiently for the company, in line with what Porter had already advocated in 1996, when he said that managers should increasingly consider companies as a whole, valuing the core competencies of key resources and clearly defining the critical success factors. It is necessary to safeguard that there are major differences between companies, but that they basically focus on the activities needed to create, produce, sell and distribute their products or services.

Thus, Porter (1986) considered that one of the factors in the proficiency of companies is how they manage costs and the advantages associated with them, in order to carry out their activity in the pursuit of full efficiency, compared to the competition in the sector, using early identification of the critical success factors, as variables that can influence the company's competitive advantage or disadvantage.

In fact, Quintella, Rocha and Alves (2005) also defended what Porter (1996) recommended when he stated that the KSFs should be considered as valid empirical variables for coherent and general use in any type of strategic business planning, since they allow and promote a clear identification of the company's objectives and, in parallel, the definition of coherent, practical and achievable strategies to be used to maintain the company's competitive advantage and its continuity in the market.

Clearly, the critical success factors, according to these authors, allow companies to strategically plan actions aimed at business success, maintaining the quality of the services provided and, as a result, satisfying their customers, increasing demand and allowing them to keep pace with the rapid evolution of today's economy.

Associated with the KSFs we find the quality of the services provided, essentially because of the importance it also has in the organizational 'balance' of any company, since it should be one of the objectives to be initially defined as a response to the search for customer satisfaction and expectations.

Following this line of thought, the concept of quality is discussed next, taking into account the literature review carried out, setting it in a historical context and then relating it to the services provided.

1.2 - Quality Assessment of Services Provided

The concept of quality has been defined in various contexts over the years. In a business context, according to Gomes (2004), it is associated with the customer's satisfaction with the product they buy or the service they contract, taking into account that it exceeds the expectations they had previously built up.

In fact, looking at the history of the evolution of this concept, it can be seen that the quality of a product or service has multiple facets and is primarily oriented towards the varying needs of customers, to which the strategies of each organization will have to be adapted (Crato, 2010). The author also believes that in order to define strategies, it will be necessary to involve and give responsibility to top management and employees by applying management based on metrics and facts, using statistical tools to control variability and emphasizing the customer.

Gomes (2004) states that in order to increase and maintain quality levels, any organization must go through several stages, namely clarifying the ideology of quality and setting up teams to implement it, as well as planning and then implementing a strategic plan that exceeds the expectations of the organization's target customers.

In this line of thought and also taking into account the evolution of the concept of quality in a business context, Oliveira (2006) identifies four major phases which are briefly discussed: inspection, statistical control, quality assurance and total quality.

According to the same author, the so-called inspection phase involved checking the product by both the producer and the customer, and was a recurring feature of the era prior to the Industrial Revolution, during which its use became more constant, at a time when there was a shift from a traditional agricultural economy to a more industrial one, where mass production emerged and the responsibility for this inspection lay with the workers themselves, who had to detect any manufacturing defects by observation alone and without using specific, previously defined techniques.

Ribeiro (2009) points out that this mass production and the type of inspection used led to a dramatic increase in defective production, contributing to the emergence of a new professional category, the quality inspector who, at the time, inspected the entire production process by task, dividing the products into defective or non-conforming and non-defective or conforming, without analyzing the causes and working to correct them.

As the industry evolved, in 1930, according to Oliveira (2006), quality inspection was considered insufficient and a technique that entailed too many costs to avoid delivering lower quality products and defrauding customers of their expectations, so the statistical control phase began, using the sampling technique for this purpose, which was nothing more than applying statistical formulas to products chosen at random from the target population and analyzed as significant samples of the same, in order to verify the quality of the product batch. At the beginning of the implementation, the basis of the work was the product itself, later evolving to the total production process, so that part of the causes of the defects found could also be verified.

In the 1960s, according to Crato (2010), the third phase in the evolution of the concept of quality began with the emergence of quality assurance, which was largely based on product differentiation strategies, valuing quality rather than quantity of production, It was at this time that the transposition of various military standards into the international arena began. The first was published in 1968 by the *American Society for Quality Control* (ASQC) and was called Generic Requirements Specifications for a Quality Program.

According to the same author, the *British Standards Institute* (BSI) developed BS 4891: A Guide to the Operation and Evaluation of Quality Assurance Systems in 1972, followed by other standards that served as the basis for the international publication of the ISO 9000 series of standards in 1987.

In Portugal, according to Crato (2010), this issue only began to gain prominence from the 1970s onwards, with its implementation becoming more concrete from the 1990s onwards, with the emphasis on quality certification, namely due to the emergence of industrial complexes such as the nuclear and petrochemical industries, whose clients demanded a guarantee of the final quality of the products, thus promoting the emergence and rapid growth of companies with quality certification.

Finally, as an evolutionary stage in quality, total quality management emerged between the 1980s and 1990s, which is nothing more than the continuous search to increase the level of quality in production and, consequently, to maintain customer satisfaction, guaranteeing its place in the market (Crato, 2010).

Ribeiro (2009) considers this stage to be the most humanized stage of the whole quality concept, since it emphasizes that the objectives of organizations have to be based on satisfying the demands of both customers and employees, i.e. all parts of the organization are responsible for guaranteeing the quality of products and services, working together as a whole to achieve the same common goal.

When analyzing the evolution of the concept of quality, it was found that it is easier to define the concept of quality when it relates to products and not services, since the history of this concept is intrinsically associated with industry, and it is also correct to say that quality is more easily identified when talking about products and more subjective when dealing with services (Crato, 2010).

In fact, the same author also points out that products are tangible goods resulting from a controlled production process that tends to become uniform in the medium term and therefore allows for the standardization of methods in order to obtain the good that is to be produced.

In the case of services, the whole process involves analyzing the service, the customer's interaction with the human resources of the company providing the desired service, as well as the context in which this interaction takes place (Crato, 2010).

Crato (2010) identifies Paladini (2000) as the main researcher who defined the characteristics of quality management in a service environment, taking into account that production and consumption are simultaneous and there is no way of defining where one ends and the other begins; that production processes do not have objective information about their operations, which are not always repeated frequently; that quality management is clearly geared towards actions that seek greater contact with the client, defining their interests, preferences, requirements, needs, conveniences, in short, everything that is considered relevant in the process of providing the service; that quality assessment focuses only on elements - there are no specific control points that can be identified; that quality management emphasizes directing the company towards a specific customer relationship model; that the service cannot have the property of making *stock*.

Taking into account the characteristics identified, Oliveira (2006) reinforces the difficulty in defining and evaluating the quality of services, which is why it is essential to know what customers expect from the service they are being provided with, presupposing constant attention to the customer, since their behavior, expectations and desires tend to change constantly.

Thus, the same author stresses that organizations can only consider their services to be of quality when they are able to continuously and constantly monitor the changes that customers are showing in their behavioral decisions.

At the same time, it is necessary to know the requirements associated with customers and to meet them or, if possible, exceed them in order to provide a quality service.

Crato (2010) even mentions the example of a case study presented at a training course on quality management in which the owner of a small, simple restaurant, seeing that his profits were increasing reasonably, decided to invest in expanding the restaurant and improving the conditions of the space, transforming what was close to a tavern into a more sophisticated restaurant. Contrary to all expectations, customers began to stop coming to the establishment, even though there had been no change in the dishes served or the price. In addition, the author concluded that in this specific case the identification of the customer's requirements and expectations and the perception by the organization (in this case, the restaurant owner) of the quality produced for the customers failed.

Obviously, the identification of customer requirements, i.e. the needs and expectations that customers want to see satisfied with the purchase of a certain good or the provision of a certain service, is one of the essential characteristics that must be met in organizations' quest for quality (Oliveira, 2006).

These requirements can be identified using various methods, including by the customers themselves through, for example, the conclusion of a contract, and are called explicit, or identified by the organization through market research, The analysis of customer feedback (such as complaints, suggestions, the results of satisfaction surveys) and the holding of periodic meetings with customers are some of the most commonly used approaches, and are referred to as implicit (Ribeiro, 2009).

In fact, what should be valued, according to the various authors mentioned above, is the customer's satisfaction after a quality service has been provided, in order to maintain it as such and ensure that they feel increasingly satisfied with the organization's services.

On the subject of satisfaction as an indicator of the quality of services provided, some fundamental concepts are discussed below.

1.3 - CUSTOMER SATISFACTION AS AN INDICATOR OF SERVICE QUALITY

According to Crato (2010), one of the difficulties in relating the quality indicator of the services provided to customer satisfaction is essentially due to the failure to identify and initially interpret customer requirements, which undermines the organization's strategy to meet the quality desired by customers, which can lead to significant economic losses for the organization.

Obviously, this phase will be essential if the result is to benefit both the organization and the customer, and it is clear that their expectations must be identified, analysed and monitored on an ongoing basis so that the organization's performance also meets them (Crato, 2010).

At the same time, according to Costa (2008), the organization must produce the quality that the customer expects, reducing the possible factors that interfere with it, namely lack of employee training, poor infrastructure maintenance conditions, breakdowns of goods needed to provide the service, failures in internal communication, among other factors.

Thus, the same author (2008) describes that a customer's satisfaction with a service only occurs when their evaluation of that service is equal to or greater than what they expected it to be, i.e. satisfaction is equal to perception minus expectation.

According to Costa (2008), it will be necessary to implement a more methodical and systemic approach that covers the entire activity of the company, so that at each stage associated with providing the service to the customer, the quality that is intended to be achieved at the end is safeguarded.

In this sense, according to Crato (2010), quality management systems aim to constantly monitor the degree of customer satisfaction with the quality of the services provided, following international quality standards, ISO 9001 being the most widely used and based on the *Demming* cycle or PDCA cycle (*Plan-Plan-Do-Check-Act*), in which the main objective is the continuous improvement of customer satisfaction in relation to the product or service offered, based on eight essential principles: Customer focus; Leadership; Involvement of people; Process approach; Management as a system approach; Continuous improvement; Fact-based decision-making approach; Mutually beneficial relationships with suppliers.

According to Neves (2003), any service provided with quality facilitates and streamlines bureaucratic-functional procedures, generates added wealth, induces an idea of rigor, restraint, justice, fairness and credibility, since organizations must be guided by these characteristics in order to remain in today's market, They need to incorporate a range of strategies into their management system, including results orientation, customer focus, leadership commitment, process adaptation, people involvement, continuous improvement and innovation, mutually beneficial partnerships and public responsibility.

1.4 - SATISFACTION *VS* IMPORTANCE

When defining the KSFs, organizations should also carry out an analysis of their position in the market, so as to be able to carry out a constant performance evaluation aimed at the pursuit of quality (Porter, 1996), always bearing in mind customer satisfaction.

Satisfaction has emerged as one of the most important resources available to companies in order to achieve and strengthen competitiveness and ensure long-term success in an increasingly competitive environment and with increasingly demanding customers (Rigopoulou, Chaniotakis, Lymperopoulos, & Siomkos, 2008). Customers who are satisfied with the purchase of a product or service are more likely to return to the company, while if they are dissatisfied they are less likely to return (Skogland & Siguaw, 2004). In this way, customer satisfaction can lead the company to boost its future business, and a satisfied customer can pass on their satisfaction to another customer, thus becoming a positive driving force for expanding the company's customer portfolio.

Satisfaction provides information for analyzing an organization's performance based on results. By comparing the importance and satisfaction of certain factors, it makes it possible to identify the areas in which to intervene and focus on service performance (Martilla & James, 1977; Matzler, Sauerwein & Heischmidt, 2003; Aktas, Aksu & Çizel, 2007; Abalo, Varela & Manzano, 2007; Silva & Fernandes, 2010).

In this context, we will now describe the management tool adapted by Matzler, Sauerwein and Heischmidt (2003), where the authors replaced the Performance dimension with Satisfaction and thus present the Importance *vs.* Satisfaction Matrix. It should be noted that this matrix was based on the instrument developed by Martilla and James (1977), where these authors measure the Importance *vs* Performance of an organization. This analysis makes it possible, through a Cartesian representation, to identify the areas where an organization should concentrate, reduce or maintain its efforts and also to assess the areas where the greatest deviations occur between what is important to the individual and what they are receiving.

The following figure shows four quadrants in the Cartesian referential, which allow us to outline four different strategies:

- Quadrant A - Concentrating efforts;
- Quadrant B - Keep up the good work;
- Quadrant C - Low priority;
- Quadrant D - Superfluous effort.

All the variables under study are also used to measure Importance *vs.* Satisfaction from the customers' point of view. This analysis assumes that there is linearity between Importance and Satisfaction and the crossing of the axes are the averages based on each dimension - Importance and Satisfaction.

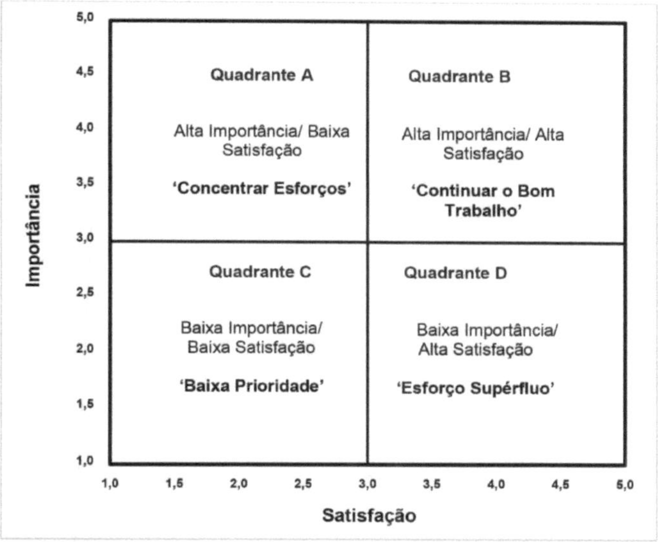

Figure 1 - Importance *vs.* satisfaction matrix.

Source: Adapted from Matzler, Sauerwein and Heischmidt (2003, p. 115).

An analysis of the figure above shows that (Martilla & James, 1977; Matzler, Sauerwein & Heischmidt, 2003; Silva & Fernandes, 2010):

- Quadrant A represents the attributes that are very important, but the level of satisfaction is rated below average. To increase overall satisfaction, the organization should focus on these attributes;
- The attributes located in quadrant B are rated with high importance and satisfaction and represent the opportunities to gain or maintain competitive advantages;

- The attributes positioned in quadrant C are considered less important and the level of satisfaction is below average. There is usually no need to focus on these attributes;
- Attributes that are in quadrant D are assessed as highly satisfactory and of low importance. This implies that the resources committed to these attributes would be better spent on others; high performance in attributes considered irrelevant indicates a possible exaggeration.

This study will use this instrument to analyze Importance *vs.* Satisfaction in the perception of Futurlab's customers.

2. RESEARCH METHODOLOGY

Taking into account the various existing research techniques and according to the study in question, the questionnaire survey was considered the most appropriate research instrument and the one with which the best results could be obtained.

This is an instrument that has been widely used in the field of Business Sciences, as it allows the researcher to collect information without being subjective (Baranano, 2004).

This research project used a questionnaire survey that had already been validated and which served as the basis for the study by the authors Wu, Tang and Shyu (2009) carried out in Japan, which aimed to identify the key success factors of the *E-Life Mall Corporation* (Taiwan). In order to validate the questionnaire survey for the Portuguese context, a direct translation was made from English into Portuguese and a back-translation into English, to check that the translation was in line with the original. Only the individual characterization variables were adapted to the Portuguese context in order to be applied to the clients of the company under study, namely the client companies of Futurlab - Material de Laboratório, Lda. This company has a wealth of experience built up over the last 30 years in the laboratory supplies and equipment trade. It has focused on innovating laboratory techniques in the fields of teaching, research and industrial control, where it has positioned itself as the market leader in laboratory equipment.

2.1 - Study Objective and Research Hypotheses

The main aim of this research is to identify and evaluate Futurlab's Critical Success Factors (CSFs) by comparing the importance given to certain factors and their respective satisfaction, based on customers' perceptions of the satisfaction/importance of the service provided by the company. The aim is also to observe the strategies that maximize customer satisfaction and to visualize the company's ability to improve its *performance in* order to keep and/or attract more customers.

Based on the study by Wu, Tang and Shyu (2009), they recognized the following critical success factors that maximized customer satisfaction compared to their direct competitor: Strategic company management; Strategy and convenience; Promotional strategy; Price competitiveness; Quality after-sales service; Information systems services; and, Corporate image.

In this context, and based on the Critical Success Factors presented in the previous paragraph, we want to see whether the same Critical Success Factors will be retained for Futurlab or whether other CSFs will be identified.

In order to verify whether the KSFs maximize customer satisfaction at Futurlab, the following research hypotheses were established:

Research Hypothesis 1: Futurlab's customers are satisfied with all the identified KSFs;

Research Hypothesis 2: There is a positive relationship between the KSFs and overall satisfaction with Futurlab.

2.2 - DATA COLLECTION INSTRUMENT

The data collection instrument is based on a questionnaire (see Appendix III) and consists of 3 parts. The first part aims to gather information on the importance attributed to the services provided by Futurlab. The second part aims to assess the level of satisfaction with the services provided by Futurlab. The third part is designed to collect information that characterizes the companies and their representatives, including questions such as gender, age, educational qualifications, position held in the company, type of company or sector of activity, number of employees, net profit, frequency of visits by Futurlab sales representatives and the company's location.

The first and second parts used qualitative variables measured on a *Likert-type* ordinal scale. The third part consists of dichotomous, multiple choice and open response questions.

The questionnaire consists of 69 variables to measure the latent variables - Critical Success Factors - such as Strategic company management, Strategy and convenience, Promotional strategy, Price competitiveness, Quality after-sales service, Information systems services, Corporate image.

To measure the importance and satisfaction of the services provided by Futurlab, a five-point *Likert* scale was used: 1 - Not at all important; 2 - Not very important; 3 - Relatively important; 4 - Very important; 5 - Extremely important; and the ordinal satisfaction scale: 1 - Very dissatisfied; 2 - Dissatisfied; 3 - Neither dissatisfied nor satisfied; 4 - Satisfied; 5 - Very satisfied.

The questionnaires were administered during the Annual Meeting of the Council of the College of Pharmaceutical Industry Specialty, which took place from March 12 to 14, 2010 in Porto, during visits to clients throughout 2010-2012, and also via email.

The company Futurlab gave permission to carry out this research work, as well as to apply the questionnaires to client companies with an official request and the respective approval given by the company's Managing Partner at the time. These documents can be found in

Appendices I and II of this paper.

2.3 - DATA PROCESSING TECHNIQUES

Once the information has been collected, it needs to be processed, analyzed and interpreted. For this purpose, the statistical *software* SPSS *Statistics* version 19 and *Microsoft Office Excel 2007* were used.

In order to respond to the objective of this study and the respective research hypotheses, it was decided to proceed with the application:

i. of the management tool - Matrix of Importance *vs.* Satisfaction;

ii. exploratory and inferential descriptive statistical techniques, to study the behavior of the attributes under study, as well as the existence of correlation or differences between the control variables and the latent variables (Satisfaction and Importance);

iii. multivariate statistical techniques, such as exploratory factor analysis to analyze the inherent structure between the variables under analysis and examine the interrelationships between them and identify the Critical Success Factors. *Cluster* analysis was also used to help classify homogeneous groups of Futurlab's client companies.

Thus, after analyzing Importance *vs.* Satisfaction, this study also uses descriptive, exploratory, inferential and multivariate analysis.

The exploratory descriptive analysis will make it possible to characterize the study sample.

In the descriptive and inferential analysis of this study, the overall aim is to verify satisfaction and importance based on the control variables Gender, Age, Academic qualifications, Position held in the company, Type of company, Net profit, Frequency of visits and Location of the company. To this end, and whenever possible, parametric tests were applied; namely the *Student's t-test to* analyze whether there are differences between the means for two independent samples, and also to analyze whether there are differences between the independent samples in relation to the latent variables under analysis (Satisfaction and Importance).

The first step was to calculate the mean for the latent variables (Importance/Satisfaction). Subsequently, in order to apply the parametric tests, the assumptions inherent to them were analyzed for two independent samples, i.e. whether the sample size was equal to or greater than thirty cases or whether the variable followed a normal distribution and whether the variances were homogeneous for independent samples, using the *Levene* test. When one of these assumptions was violated, a non-parametric test was used as an alternative to the parametric test, for two independent samples. Both assumptions had to be met for three or more independent samples, so for different situations the *Kruskal-Wallis* test had to be applied.

The aim of multivariate analysis is to obtain results on the importance of certain Critical Success Factors in companies and their degree of satisfaction with the company under study, using Exploratory Factor Analysis and Cluster Analysis to identify homogeneous groups of customers.

Factor analysis is an exploratory data analysis that aims to discover and analyze the structure of a set of interrelated variables in order to construct a measurement scale for factors that in some way control the original variables. In principle, if two variables are correlated, this association results from sharing a common characteristic that is not directly observable (Marôco, 2010). Thus, the primary objective of this analysis is to assign a quantification to factors that are not directly observable. In this way, factor analysis produces a quantification that weights highly correlated responses. This quantification makes it possible to summarize the information present in many variables into a small number of factors that are not directly observable (Marôco, 2010).

The sample in this study complies with the minimum sample size rules for the use of factor analysis, as Hill and Hill (2009) suggest that the minimum sample is 5 cases per item observed.

According to the same authors, it is important to analyze the reliability of the questionnaire used to measure the latent variable, as conclusions can only be drawn from a measure that has adequate reliability. The first test to be carried out to determine the reliability of the instrument used should be *Cronbach's Alpha*, which measures the reliability and quality of the instrument, assessing the degree of internal consistency between multiple measures of a variable (Churchill, 1979).

Thus, in this study, a *Cronbach's alpha* of 0.898 was obtained for the Importance analysis, which is between 0.8 and 0.9 and is considered Good, and a *Cronbach's alpha of* 0.910 was recorded for the Satisfaction analysis, which is above 0.9 and is considered Very Good. Therefore, according to Marôco (2010), the internal consistency of the questionnaire used was good.

However, in order to apply factor analysis, there still needs to be a correlation between the variables. This is because if the correlations are small, there is a chance that they do not share factors and therefore this analysis would not make sense. The calculation of the

Kaiser-Meyer-Olkin (KMO) measure together with *Bartlett*'s test of sphericity are the two statistical tests that make it possible to check the quality of the correlations between variables in order to give confidence in the analysis going forward. The KMO is a measure of the adequacy of the sample that varies between 0 and 1, which compares the simple correlations with the partial correlations observed between variables. This makes it possible to check whether there is a strong correlation between variables. *Bartlett*'s test of sphericity tests the hypothesis that the correlation matrix is an identity matrix with a determinant equal to 1, thus showing whether or not there is a correlation between the variables (Marôco, 2010).

Another analysis to carry out is group or *cluster* analysis. This is an exploratory multivariate analysis technique that makes it possible to group subjects or variables into homogeneous groups with regard to one or more common characteristics. Identifying natural groupings of subjects or variables makes it possible to assess the dimensionality of the data matrix, identify possible multivariate *outliers* and raise hypotheses about the structural relationships between variables. In this type of analysis, subjects and/or variables are grouped based on measures of similarity or dissimilarity between subjects or two *clusters of* observations, using hierarchical or non-hierarchical *cluster* grouping techniques (Marôco, 2010). The number of *clusters (k)* cannot be greater than the number of variables (*p*), and usually *k* is much smaller than *p* (Hill & Hill, 2009).

A significance level of 5% will be used throughout the analysis to make decisions on the different research hypotheses.

2.4 - BRIEF CHARACTERIZATION OF THE STUDY POPULATION AND SAMPLE

The study population is based on the universe of customers who are loyal to Futurlab as a supplier of laboratory equipment. These include schools, external laboratories for water and food analysis, among others, the pharmaceutical industry, the food industry, among others. It should also be noted that we also wanted to analyze what function the respondent had in the company and what their gender was. In other words, every analysis is based on the response of the manager of Futurlab's client company.

In the 2010-2012 period under analysis, a total of 1,055 Futurlab customers were randomly surveyed, of which only 225 answered the questionnaire, representing 21% of the population under study and according to the distribution shown in the table below.

To calculate the sample size, a sampling error of 5.8% and a significance level of 5% were assumed. It should be noted that in Table 1, the relative frequency calculation for the sample size by sector took into account the universe of that sector.

The following table shows a curious fact: of the 40 external laboratories, all responded to the questionnaire, of the 140 food companies, 40 responded to the questionnaire, representing 29% of the sample, 17% of the sample is from the pharmaceutical industry and 36% are teaching schools or research laboratories.

Table 1 - Population *vs.* Sample.

Sector	Population		Sample	
	N	%	n	%
Pharmacy	166	16%	29	17%
Industrial control	129	12%	17	13%
Cryopreservation	10	1%	0	-
Food	140	13%	40	29%
External Laboratory	40	4%	40	100%
Teaching/research	147	14%	53	36%
Others	423	40%	46	11%
Total	**1055**	**100%**	**225**	**21%**

2.5 - SAMPLE CHARACTERIZATION AND DEFINITION

The following table shows that Futurlab's clients are mainly education/research with 23.6% of responses, followed by the food industry and external laboratories with 17.8%. The Pharmaceutical Industry is also highly represented, with 12.9%.

Table 2 - Type of company or sector of activity.

	Sample	%
Pharmaceutical Industry	29	12,9
Industrial Control	17	7,6
Food industry	40	17,8
External laboratories (water, food,...)	40	17,8
Teaching/Research	53	23,6
Others	46	20,4
Total	**225**	**100**

As can be seen in the figure below, the majority of respondents are located in the Lisbon and Tagus Valley area with 58.2% of respondents, followed by Porto and the North with 17.8% of responses. In this case, only 3 respondents did not answer, representing a total of 1.3%.

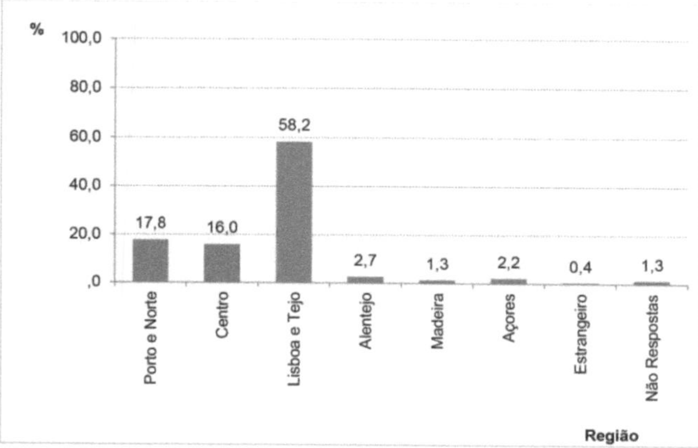

Figura 2 - Location of respondents.

As can be seen from the table below, Futurlab's client companies are essentially small and medium-sized enterprises with between 10 and 50 employees, with 28.9% of the 183 individuals who answered this question, and 42 companies not answering this question.

Table 3 - Number of company employees.

Scale of employees	Frequency	%
Less than or equal to 10 employees	25	13,7
Between 11 and 50	65	35,5
Between 51 and 100	55	30,1
Between 101 and 500	27	14,8
Between 501 and 1000	4	2,2
Greater than or equal to 1001	7	3,8
Total	**183**	**100**

It should be noted that large companies are also represented, with a total of 7 out of 225, which corresponds to 3.8% of all respondents.

Figure 3 shows the companies' annual net profit in euros. This question became a sensitive variable because 57% of the companies didn't answer and 34% of the valid answers have a net profit of more than €55,001 a year.

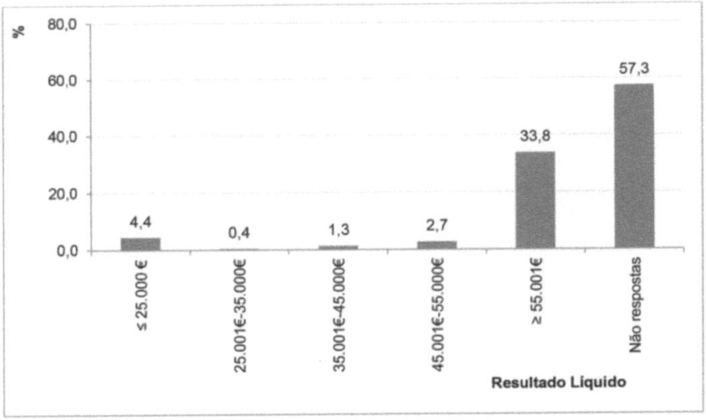

Figura 3 - Annual Net Profit, in euros.

With regard to the gender of the individuals who were surveyed, being the managers of Futurlab's client company, the following figure shows that the majority are female, 61%, and 39% male. It's interesting to see this significant percentage corresponding to the female sex, so we can observe the tendency for the female sex to increasingly take on management roles or be responsible for departments.

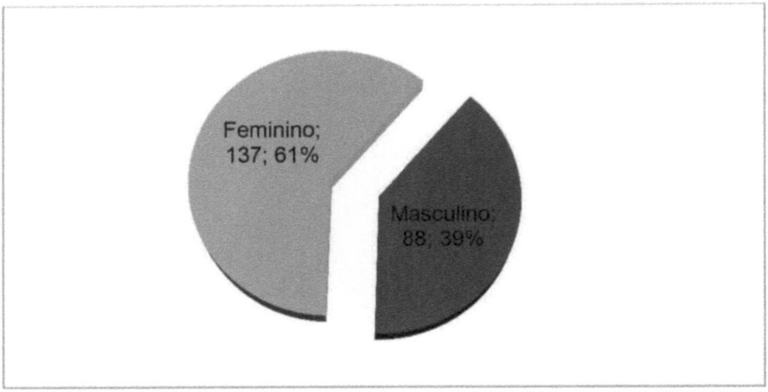

Figure 4 - Distribution of respondents by gender.

As can be seen in Table 4, the majority of respondents are young people, between the ages of 31 and 35, accounting for 24.9% of respondents. It can also be seen that 93.8% of the individuals are aged 50 or under. Only 6.2% are over 50. Of the total number of respondents, only 0.9% correspond to 2 individuals aged over 56.

Table 4 - Age of Respondents, by class interval.

Age group	Frequency	%
Under or equal to 25 years old	7	3,1
Between 26 and 30 years old	34	15,1
Between 31 and 35 years old	56	24,9
Between 36 and 40 years old	41	18,2
Between 41 and 45 years old	43	19,1
Between 46 and 50 years old	30	13,3
Between 51 and 55 years old	12	5,3
56 years or older	2	0,9
Total	**225**	**100,0**

The following figure shows the educational qualifications of the respondents, the majority of whom have a bachelor's degree (53.3%), corresponding to a total of 120 respondents. There is also a high percentage of respondents with a master's degree, with 25.3% (57 respondents).

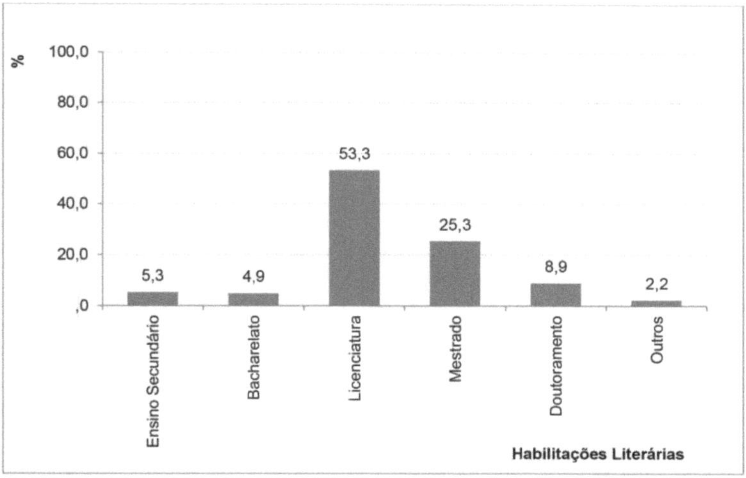

Figura 5 - Literary Skills.

Figure 6 shows the positions held by the respondents in the company. 33.8% are laboratory technicians, 12.4% are purchasing technicians and 9.3% are laboratory directors. Then, in smaller numbers, there are Professors, Quality Managers, Managers, Research Fellows, Managers, among others.

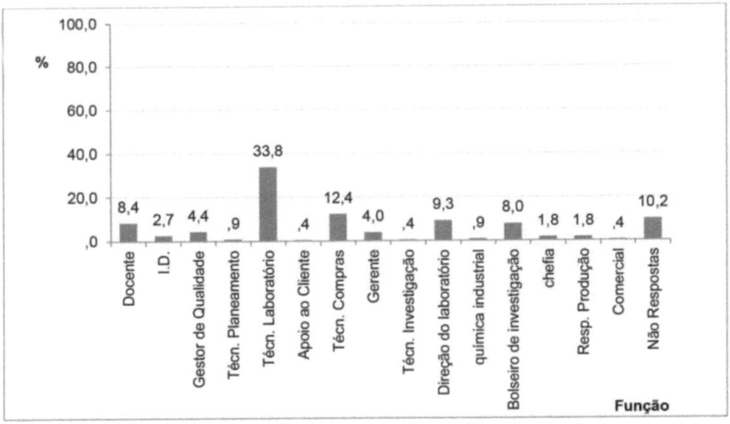

Figura 6 - Position held in the company.

Figure 7 shows the frequency of visits by Futurlab sales staff to the client companies surveyed. From the analysis, it can be seen that the regularity with which sales representatives visit client companies more than once a month is 46%, while 28% visit every month and 22% every two weeks. It should be noted that only 4% of those surveyed visit every week.

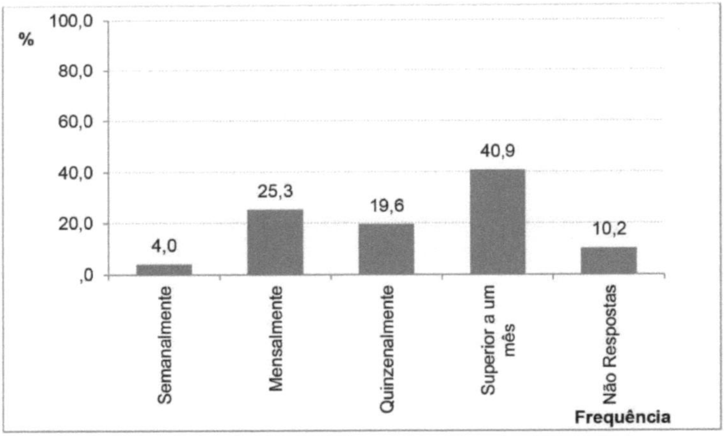

Figura 7 - Frequency of visits.

In this question, the figure above shows that 10.2% of respondents did not answer, so the percentages above refer to the weight of respondents who answered, 202, with the total sample being 225.

3. IDENTIFICATION OF CRITICAL SUCCESS FACTORS IN THE DEVELOPMENT OF STRATEGIES THAT MAXIMIZE CUSTOMER SATISFACTION

3.1 - Exploratory and Inferential Descriptive Analysis

In order to respond to the objective of this study, this section aims to carry out an exploratory descriptive analysis of the information collected through the questionnaire survey, as well as an inferential analysis.

To get a simple idea of whether the control variables have been answered, the results shown in Table 5 can be analyzed.

It can be seen that only two questions became sensitive, such as the company's net profit, where only 96 of the 225 respondents answered the question, as well as the question that would control the number of employees in the company, which only 183 of the 225 respondents answered.

Looking at the control variables, it can be seen that the annual net profit of the companies is a variable to which many people did not respond, 57.33% of the respondents (Table 5).

Table 5 - Summary of overall descriptive statistics for the control variables.

Control variables	Valid	% Valid	No answers	% no answers
Type of company or sector of activity	225	100	0	-
Location	222	98,67	3	1,33
Gender	225	100	0	-
Age	225	100	0	-
Literary Skills	225	100	0	-
Position held in the company	202	89,78	23	10,22
No. of company employees	183	81,33	42	18,67
Net Profit (€)	96	42,67	129	57,33
Frequency of commercial visits	202	89,78	23	10,22
County	222	98,67	3	1,33

The 225 responses to the latent variables that make up our questionnaire are always obtained, which helps us to draw more realistic conclusions about the sample in question.

Since satisfaction and importance are being analyzed, the data collected should be analyzed in two different ways for Satisfaction and Importance. The total score in each table shows the attitude of each respondent towards the KSFs, which is more favorable the higher the score (see Table 8 and 10).

In the analysis of importance (Table 6), the variables 2, 3, 13 and 19 stand out (see Table 6). Items 2 and 3 evaluate the same component in relation to the company's strategic management, while item number 13 evaluates the component on price competitiveness and item 19 evaluates after-sales services. In other words, this shows a clear position of consumers in relation to the components, attributing importance to the various areas.

The items with the worst results are 12 and 17 (see Table 6) because they are related to the promotional strategy component and quality after-sales service respectively, so it can be concluded that the respondents attach importance to these items.

It should be noted that the standard deviation values are low, which allows us to conclude that there is a concentration of responses around the average, with no dispersion of results.

Table 6 - Results of the items in relation to the latent variable Importance (n=225).

	ITEM	NI	PI	IR	MI	EI	Average	Standard Deviation
I1	Suitable warehouse/store close to customer sites	18	41	91	65	10	3,04	,986
I2	Adequate supply of products	0	0	12	80	133	4,54	,597
I3	Accurate and efficient distribution logistics	0	0	12	94	119	4,48	,598
I4	Development of a virtual distribution channel	7	24	104	66	24	3,34	,917
I5	Having a variety of products in stock	0	5	53	112	55	3,96	,755
I6	Rapid replacement of products and placing new products on the market	0	19	38	126	42	3,85	,821
I7	Unique amenities	0	37	92	85	11	3,31	,802
I8	Having an organized and well-presented display and distribution of products	0	32	15	146	32	3,79	,859
I9	Creative promotional strategies for integrating both virtual and practical channels	6	20	120	47	32	3,35	,924
I10	Promotional activities for occasional congresses/seminars	9	30	120	63	3	3,09	,788
I11	Intense promotional or discount activities	6	22	62	76	54	3,68	1,037

I12	A membership card system with a free or low-income membership	28	72	69	51	5	2,70	1,024
I13	Cheaper and more competitive products	0	0	34	66	125	4,40	,739
I14	Cheap maintenance and accessories	0	5	33	93	94	4,23	,778
I15	Easy to interpret quotes with all the information you need	0	0	18	108	99	4,36	,626
I16	Money-back guarantee if found cheaper	3	40	79	62	41	3,44	1,025
I17	Free 24-hour telephone service	19	56	72	63	15	3,00	1,067
I18	Free maintenance services	9	28	32	97	59	3,75	1,098
I19	Delivery services to the customer's premises	0	6	11	91	117	4,42	,709
I20	Installation services at the client company's premises	0	6	35	78	106	4,26	,817
I21	Easy access to information on the activities of the supplier/distributor company	19	12	90	69	35	3,40	1,081
I22	Maintenance products for the home delivery service	10	6	91	93	25	3,52	,892
I23	*Online* professional advice	0	27	85	72	41	3,56	,924
I24	Providing *online* services such as product displays and price searches	0	12	39	83	91	4,12	,883
I25	Easy and convenient *online* services	6	6	31	88	94	4,15	,941
I26	Suggestions and customer information calls	6	33	74	94	18	3,38	,923
I27	A reputable and credible company	0	12	11	119	83	4,21	,767
I28	Healthy financial position	0	6	65	102	52	3,89	,786
I29	Social activities within the community	11	19	137	58	0	3,08	,731
I30	Clarifying the company's mission	6	27	112	74	6	3,21	,788

Note: 1 - Not at all important (NI); 2 - Not very important (PI); 3 - Relatively important (RI); 4 - Very important (MI); 5 - Extremely important (EI).

With regard to Overall Importance on the scale as well as in the different components, it can be seen that the empirical averages obtained score above the theoretical values (indifference position) (see Table **7**), which reveals the importance that the respondents attach to the critical success factors analyzed.

The standard deviation for each latent variable shows very small values, which reveals a reasonable agreement in the answers obtained around the empirical average. It should be noted that the maximum values achieved by components in some situations reached the maximum possible and in others they were very close to the maximum possible. However, for overall importance, the maximum possible is higher than the empirical maximum.

Table 7 - Statistical summary for each component (FCS) for the latent variable Importance.

Components (FCS)	Minimum	Maximo	Empirical Average	Deviation Standard	Maximo Possible	Average Theoretical	*Z-Score*
Quality after-sales service	15,00	27,00	22,34	3,37	30,00	18,00	1,29
Price competitiveness	11,00	20,00	16,43	2,49	20,00	12,00	1,78
Strategic company management	10,00	20,00	15,39	1,94	20,00	12,00	1,74
Information Systems Services	8,00	20,00	15,21	2,86	20,00	12,00	1,12
Corporate image	7,00	19,00	14,39	2,33	20,00	12,00	1,02
Convenience Strategy	9,00	19,00	14,92	2,29	20,00	12,00	1,27
Promotional Strategy	4,00	18,00	12,76	2,72	20,00	12,00	0,28
Global importance	**77,00**	**133,00**	**111,31**	**13,17**	**150,00**	**90,00**	**1,62**

The following table shows the values obtained for each item under analysis for the latent variable Satisfaction.

Thus, in the analysis of the latent variable Satisfaction, items 19, 2 and 15 stand out (Table 8), with high values, which shows that the respondents are satisfied with these items provided by Futurlab. Item 19 evaluates the after-sales service and item 2 evaluates the component relating to the company's strategic management, while item number 15 evaluates the component on price competitiveness.

The items with the worst results are 12, 17 and 29 (Table 8) and are related to the promotional strategy component and quality after-sales service and corporate image, respectively.

The standard deviation was also low for each of the items presented, which shows that the answers obtained are in agreement with the average.

Table 8 - Results of the items in relation to the latent variable Satisfaction (n=225).

	ITEM	MI	I	NS/NI	S	MS	Average	Standard Deviation
S1	Suitable warehouse/store close to customer sites	15	11	126	60	13	3,20	,881
S2	Adequate supply of products	0	6	50	130	39	3,90	,703
S3	Accurate and efficient distribution logistics	0	4	70	104	47	3,86	,758

S4	Development of a virtual distribution channel	3	28	137	45	12	3,16	,755
S5	Having a variety of products in stock.	0	10	85	75	55	3,78	,868
S6	Rapid replacement of products and placing new products on the market	0	18	94	57	26	3,54	,802
S7	Unique amenities	0	33	148	39	5	3,07	,637
S8	Having an organized and well-presented display and distribution of products	0	15	117	88	5	3,37	,642
S9	Creative promotional strategies for integrating both virtual and practical channels	0	10	145	58	12	3,32	,644
S10	Promotional activities for occasional congresses/seminars	6	17	171	20	11	3,06	,682
S11	Intense promotional or discount activities	0	42	115	52	16	3,19	,819
S12	A membership card system with a free or low-income membership	12	47	143	17	6	2,81	,756
S13	Cheaper and more competitive products	14	27	87	42	55	3,43	1,163
S14	Cheap maintenance and accessories	8	21	112	59	25	3,32	,918
S15	Easy to interpret quotes with all the information you need	0	16	40	123	46	3,88	,810
S16	Money-back guarantee if found cheaper	17	24	137	32	15	3,02	,906
S17	Free 24-hour telephone service	5	49	130	29	12	2,97	,807
S18	Free maintenance services	5	44	111	46	19	3,13	,901
S19	Delivery services to the customer's premises	0	11	40	70	104	4,19	,897
S20	Installation services at the client company's premises	0	11	90	63	61	3,77	,905
S21	Easy access to information on the activities of the supplier/distributor company	13	25	91	85	11	3,25	,926
S22	Maintenance products for the home delivery service	7	23	149	46	0	3,04	,657
S23	*Online* professional advice	0	29	139	39	18	3,20	,764
S24	Providing *online* services such as product displays and price searches	0	42	108	39	36	3,31	,954
S25	Easy and convenient *online* services	0	27	119	40	39	3,40	,912
S26	Suggestions and customer information calls	0	41	134	50	0	3,04	,636
S27	A reputable and credible company	0	6	72	147	0	3,63	,537
S28	Healthy financial position	0	6	134	85	0	3,35	,531

S29 Social activities within the community	6	24	164	31	0	2,98	,593
S30 Clarifying the company's mission	6	6	165	48	0	3,13	,575

Note: 1 - Very Dissatisfied (MI); 2 - Dissatisfied (I); 3 - Neither Satisfied nor Dissatisfied (NS/NI); 4 - Satisfied (S); 5 - Very Satisfied (MS).

With regard to Overall Satisfaction on the scale and in the different components, it can be seen that the averages obtained are above the theoretical values (Table 9). From this analysis it can be seen that Futurlab's customers are satisfied with the company's different activities, namely the quality after-sales service, followed by the company's strategic management and convenience strategy; on the other hand, they are less satisfied with the promotional strategy.

Here again, the values presented for the standard deviation for each component are very small, which shows agreement in the answers obtained.

It should be noted that the maximum values achieved by component and also in Overall Satisfaction are close to the maximum possible, and it can be said that satisfactory values were obtained.

Table 9 - Statistical summary for each component (FCS) for the latent variable Satisfaction.

Components (FCS)	Minimum	Maximo	Average Empirical	Deviation Standard	Maximo Possible	Average Theoretical	*Z-Score*
Quality after-sales service	10,00	28,00	20,36	3,58	30,00	18,00	0,66
Strategic company management	10,00	19,00	14,12	1,89	20,00	12,00	1,12
Convenience Strategy	9,00	18,00	13,76	2,16	20,00	12,00	0,81
Price competitiveness	5,00	19,00	13,65	3,01	20,00	12,00	0,55
Corporate image	7,00	16,00	13,09	1,78	20,00	12,00	0,61
Information Systems Services	8,00	19,00	12,86	2,62	20,00	12,00	0,33
Promotional Strategy	8,00	19,00	12,38	2,06	20,00	12,00	0,18
Overall satisfaction	**66,00**	**125,00**	**100,30**	**12,49**	**150,00**	**90,00**	**0,83**

In order to complete the analysis, we decided to check the relationship between the Importance and Satisfaction components and Global Importance and Global Satisfaction. It should be noted that the assumption of normality for applying *Pearson*'s correlation coefficient was not violated.

The correlations between the components of Importance and Overall Importance were analyzed (Table 10), and all the values presented are statistically significant at a 5% significance level. It can be seen that the component with the highest correlation is the Quality After-Sales Services component with a correlation value of 0.854 (Table 10), which is the component with the greatest weight in customer importance.

The correlation that has the least weight in relation to Global Importance is the company's strategic management with a value of 0.614 (Table 10).

The correlation between variables with the least weight is price competitiveness and the company's promotional strategy, with a value of 0.282 (Table 10). In this case, it can be inferred that this correlation has little influence on the importance of customers in relation to the company under study.

Table 10 - Correlations (*Pearson)* between components and the latent variable Global Importance.

	Strategic Company Management	Convenience Strategy	Promotional Strategy	Price competitiveness	Services Post-Quality sales	Information Systems Services	Corporate image	Global importance
Management Company strategy	1	,573	,420	,322	,318	,308	,380	,614
Convenience Strategy		1	,347	,375	,511	,410	,368	,693
Promotional Strategy			1	,282	,612	,599	,436	,751
Price competitiveness				1	,549	,323	,376	,642
Quality after-sales service					1	,631	,505	,854
Information Systems Services						1	,429	,760
Corporate image							1	,685
Global importance								1

Note: All values are statistically significant at a 5% significance level.

The correlations between the components for Satisfaction and Overall Satisfaction (Table 11) were also analyzed, showing that the components with the highest correlation are the Price Competitiveness and Quality After-Sales Services components, with a correlation value of 0.808 (Table 11), i.e. they are the components with the greatest weight in customer satisfaction.

The correlation with the lowest weight in relation to Global Satisfaction is Corporate Image with a value of 0.642 (Table 11).

The correlation between variables with the least weight is Information systems services and the company's strategic management, with a value of 0.236 (Table 11). In this case, it can be inferred that this correlation has little influence on customer satisfaction with the company under study.

Table 11 - *Pearson* correlation between components and the latent variable Global Satisfaction.

	Strategic Business Management	Convenience Strategy	Promotional Strategy	Price competitiveness	After-sales services Quality sales	Information Systems Services	Corporate image	Overall satisfaction
Management Company strategy	1	,582	,411	,567	,297	,236	,556	,670
Convenience Strategy		1	,489	,584	,440	,363	,322	,730
Promotional Strategy			1	,472	,530	,328	,329	,692
Price competitiveness				1	,547	,454	,363	,808
Quality after-sales service					1	,539	,489	,808
Services Information Systems						1	,376	,677
Corporate image							1	,642
Overall satisfaction								1

Note: All values are statistically significant at a 5% significance level.

In order to complete the analysis and check whether there were any differences in Global Satisfaction and Global Importance, based on the control variables, some parametric tests were applied and when this was not possible, non-parametric tests were used, as explained above in the research methodology section.

The following table shows the results obtained for the value of evidence and it can be seen, taking into account the most relevant ones, that: there is sufficient statistical evidence to affirm that at least one of the distributes for Overall Satisfaction in the age and job title groups is different, and the same is true for Overall Importance. The type of company or sector of activity and the company location variable have a different effect on Overall Satisfaction. For the variables company location, educational qualifications, net profit, frequency of visits and gender, there are no statistically significant differences in the responses in relation to Overall Satisfaction and Overall Importance.

Table 12 - Inferential analysis by latent variable and control variable.

Control variable	Test	Overall satisfaction (*p-value*)	Global Importance (*p-value*)
Sex	*t-Student*	0,083	0,396
Age	*Kruskal-Wallis*	<0,001	0,002
Literary Skills	*Kruskal-Wallis*	0,303	0,648
Position held in the company	*Kruskal-Wallis*	0,025	0,023
Type of company	*Kruskal-Wallis*	<0,001	0,058
Net Profit	*Kruskal-Wallis*	0,367	0,864
Frequency of visits	*Kruskal-Wallis*	0,925	0,263
Company location	*Kruskal-Wallis*	0,001	0,142

So, in general, from the values obtained for the test value and shown in the table above, it can be said that the variables age, position held in the company, type of company and its location are the ones that contribute to the existence of statistically significant differences in the satisfaction and importance given to the factors of the company under study by Futurlab's customers.

3.2 - IMPORTANCE *VS.* SATISFACTION ANALYSIS

This section aims to assess Importance *vs.* Satisfaction, based on the 7 KSFs identified in the study by Wu, Tang and Shyu (2009). To this end, the matrix adapted by Matzler et al. (2003) was used, as mentioned in point 1.4 of this paper. This study was therefore based on an analysis of the 7 KSFs and the different variables (attributes) that support the respective KSFs and which are an integral part of the questionnaire (see Appendix III).

Table 13 shows the results obtained for each attribute and for the latent variables Importance and Satisfaction, both measured on a *Likert* scale, from 1 to 5, where 1 is the most negative extreme and 5 the most positive.

According to this table, the attributes that customers mentioned as being the most important and consequently the ones with the highest averages are: Cheaper and more competitive products; Cheap maintenance and accessories; Easy-to-interpret quotes with all the information; Guaranteed refund if found cheaper; Suitable warehouse/store close to customers' premises; Adequate supply of products; Accurate and efficient distribution logistics; Development of a virtual distribution channel; Online professional advice (online consultancy); Availability of *online* services such as product presentations and price searches; Easy and convenient to use *online services and* links to suggestions and customer information.

On the other hand, the attribute with the lowest value, i.e. the item with the least importance for Futurlab's customers, was the item A membership card system with a free or low return membership (mean 2.7 and standard deviation 1.024).

When it came to evaluating the quality of the services provided by Futurlab, the attributes with the highest levels of satisfaction were Strategic management of the company, Convenience strategy and then Competitiveness of prices.

In general, the aspects considered most negative are related to the company's promotional strategy, as it is the attribute considered least important and curiously the one that customers like the least in satisfactory terms.

The values obtained for the standard deviation are considered to be low, the variations in the answers are low, but there are some that registered significant discrepancy values. This measure of dispersion reflects the variation of a set of data around the average, i.e. the greater or lesser variability of the results obtained. It allows us to identify the extent to which the results are or are not concentrated around the central tendency of a set of observations.

Thus, with regard to Importance *vs.* Satisfaction, the attributes that showed significant discrepancy values were: Cheaper and more competitive products, Cheap maintenance and accessories and Easy access to information on the activities of the supplier/distributor company.

Table 13 - Summary of the results of the Importance *vs.* Satisfaction Analysis.

Attributes and FCS	Importance		Satisfaction	
-	Average	Standard Deviation	Average	Standard Deviation
1 - Strategic Company Management				
1 i Suitable warehouse/store near 'customer premises' areas	3,04	0,986	3,20	0,881
1.2 Adequate supply of products	4,54	0,597	3,90	0,703

1.3 Have accurate and efficient distribution logistics	4,48	0,598	3,86	0,758
1.4 Designing a virtual distribution channel	3,34	0,917	3,16	0,755
2 - Convenience Strategy				
2.1 Have a variety of products in stock	3,96	0,755	3,78	0,868
2 2 Quick replacement of products and placement of 2.2 new products on the market	3,85	0,821	3,54	0,802
2.3 Unique amenities	3,31	0,802	3,07	0,637
2 4 Display and distribute products 2.4 organized and well presented	3,79	0,859	3,37	0,642
3 - Promotional strategy				
3 1 Creative promotional strategies for integrating both virtual and practical channels	3,35	0,924	3,32	0,644
_ *A* Promotional activities for congresses/seminars 3.2 occasional	3,09	0,788	3,06	0,682
3.3 Intense promotion or discount activities	3,68	1,037	3,19	0,819
34 A membership card system with a free or low-income membership	2,70	1,024	2,81	0,756
4 - Price competitiveness				
4.1 Cheaper and more competitive products	4,40	0,739	3,43	1,163
4.2 Maintenance and cheap accessories	4,23	0,778	3,32	0,918
. _ Easy to interpret quotes with all the 4.3 information	4,36	0,626	3,88	0,810
4 4 Money-back guarantee if found cheaper	3,44	1,025	3,02	0,906
5 - Quality after-sales service				
5.1 Free 24-hour telephone service	3,00	1,067	2,97	0,807
5.2 Free maintenance services	3,75	1,098	3,13	0,901
Delivery services to the company's premises client	4,42	0,709	4,19	0,897
Installation services at the company's premises client	4,26	0,817	3,77	0,905
5 5 Easy access to information about the company's activities supplier/distributor	3,40	1,081	3,25	0,926
Maintenance products for the 5.6 delivery service	3,52	0,892	3,04	0,657

home				
6 - Information Systems Services				
Professional advice *online* (Consultancy *online*)	3,56	0,924	3,20	0,764
6.2 *Online* services such as product presentation and price research	4,12	0,883	3,31	0,954
6.3 *Online* services that are easy and convenient to use	4,15	0,941	3,40	0,912
6.4 Calls for suggestions and to keep customer information	3,38	0,923	3,04	0,636
7 - Corporate image				
7.1 A reputable and credible company	4,21	0,767	3,63	0,537
7.2 Healthy financial position	3,89	0,786	3,35	0,531
7.3 Social activities within the community	3,08	0,731	2,98	0,593
7.4 Clarifying the company's mission	3,21	0,788	3,13	0,575

In order to assess the importance that customers attach to the different KSFs under analysis, as well as their level of satisfaction with Futurlab, the averages and standard deviations were calculated for the aggregate results.

The results of the survey are reflected in Table 14, according to the averages. In terms of importance, all the attributes had an average score close to or above 4 (from relatively important to very important on the *Likert* scale), ranging from 3.207 to 4.107. The three attributes considered most important were: Price competitiveness (average of 4.107 and standard deviation of 0.792), Strategic Company Management (average of 3.847 and standard deviation of 0.775), Information Systems Services (average of 3.803 and standard deviation of 0.918). The attribute considered least important was Promotional Strategy (mean of 3.207 and standard deviation of 0.943).

These results generally show low standard deviation values. Therefore, in this case, the discrepancy between the answers is considered to be low.

Based on the values shown in Table 14 and the degree of satisfaction on the part of the company, the averages and standard deviations were also calculated. The average of the satisfaction attributes varies between 3.094 and 3.529, with the average responses ranging from 3 - Neither Dissatisfied nor Satisfied to 4 - Satisfied, according to the *Likert* scale used. It can be said that the average values are satisfactory since they are always higher than the intermediate value of 3. These results lead us to conclude that, in general, customers are satisfied with Futurlab's performance, since the average of all the aggregate variables is higher than the middle value.

Table 14 - Customer opinion on the Importance *vs.* Satisfaction of the KSFs for Futurlab.

Importance				Satisfaction		
Components/FCS	Average	Standard Deviation	*Ranking*	Average	Standard Deviation	*Ranking*
Strategic Company Management	3,847	0,775	2	3,529	0,774	1
Convenience Strategy	3,729	0,809	4	3,439	0,737	2
Promotional Strategy	3,207	0,943	7	3,094	0,725	7
Price competitiveness	4,107	0,792	1	3,413	0,950	3
Quality after-sales service	3,724	0,944	5	3,393	0,849	4
Information Systems Services	3,803	0,918	3	3,239	0,816	6
Corporate image	3,597	0,768	6	3,272	0,559	5
Global Average	**3,716**	**0,850**	-	**3,340**	**0,773**	-

Also, from an analysis of the values in the table above, the attributes with the highest satisfaction, considering those with an average value above the global average, were 3. 1st place in the *ranking* went to Strategic Company Management, 2nd place to Convenience Strategy and finally to Price competitiveness. Promotional Strategy was the attribute with the lowest customer satisfaction.

In general, these results also show low standard deviation values, considering that the discrepancy between the answers is low.

The Importance *vs.* Satisfaction analysis, as already mentioned, can be done by analyzing the quadrants. Figure 8 shows the distribution and positioning of the 30 attributes analyzed in Table 13.

The positioning of the attributes was first analyzed by working the axes of the matrix with the theoretical averages (3;3). However, it turned out that most of the attributes were positioned in quadrant B - Keep up the good work. Knowing from the outset that for some attributes the company had unfavorable values for the latent variables Importance *vs.* Satisfaction, it was decided to use the average of the answers obtained for the latent variables under analysis.

From the analysis in Figure 8, special attention should be paid to the attribute in quadrant A, as it warns of the need to focus efforts on improving free maintenance services. This is a highly important attribute and one where dissatisfaction is evident. A large proportion of the attributes are in quadrant B, which is a good sign for the company.

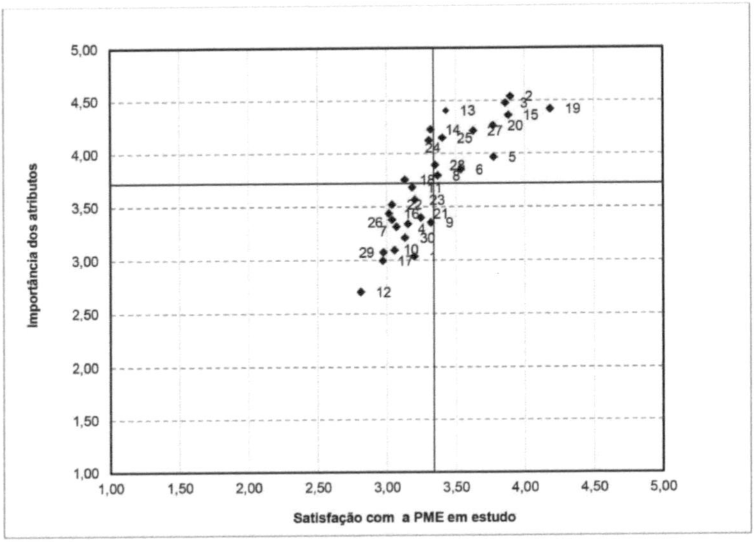

Figura 8 - Analysis of the quadrants for the attributes, for the global averages with axis on the averages (3.34;3.72).

However, the analysis presented and explained above was based on the middle points of the scales and not on the trends (median values) obtained from the results of the questionnaires.

It is therefore essential to carry out a quadrant analysis based on the overall median values for the axes, in order to see the trend of the attributes, according to Lynch, Carver, and Virgo (1996) and Martilla and James (1977).

The next figure shows the positioning of the attributes, now based on the median values. We can thus see four different quadrants from the previous ones (Figure 9), with the axis now defined by the overall median values (3.26;3.73) and the overall averages for the attributes.

Figure 9 shows how the 30 attributes under study are distributed in the Importance *vs.* Satisfaction matrix and the average of the responses. It is clear which attributes the company performs well on. There are 14 attributes out of the 30, with 6 of the 7 latent variables in quadrant B and no promotional strategy variables (virtual channels, promotions/congresses, discounts, points card).

There is only one variable in quadrant A: free maintenance services and this is a point for improvement, as it is a highly important attribute where dissatisfaction is evident. This situation had already been observed when analyzing the values shown in Figure 8.

There are also 14 attributes in quadrant C. However, this is a low priority for the company.

In quadrant D, there is also only one attribute: creative promotional strategies for integrating virtual channels as practical and this is proving to be a superfluous effort for the company.

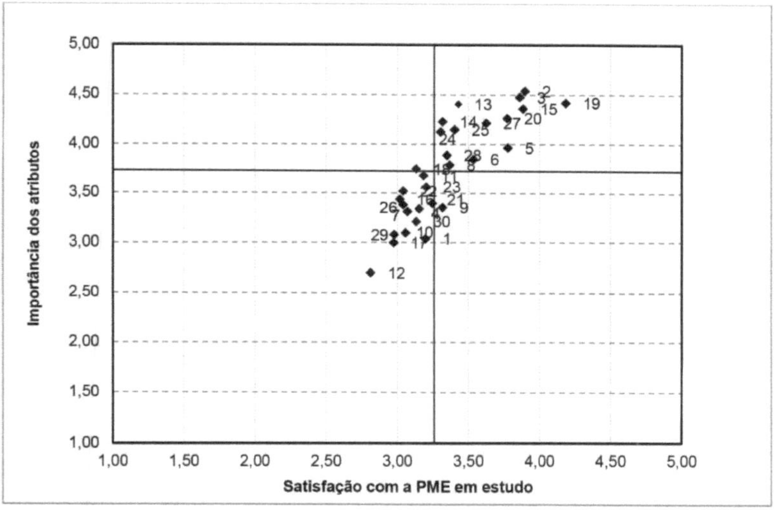

Figura 9 - Analysis of the quadrants for the attributes, for the overall averages with the axis at the
medians (3.26;3.73).

By grouping the 30 attributes into their proposed KSFs and presented in the original questionnaire and in an analogous way, the Importance *vs.* Satisfaction matrix is applied to the following KSFs: Strategic management of the company, Convenience strategy, Promotional strategy, Price competitiveness, Quality after-sales service, Information systems services, Corporate image.

It can be seen that the promotional strategy is the KSF considered least important and, curiously, the one that satisfies customers the least. Analysis of the Importance *vs.* Satisfaction matrix shows that the KSFs are mostly in quadrant B - Keep up the good work, which is a good indicator for the company.

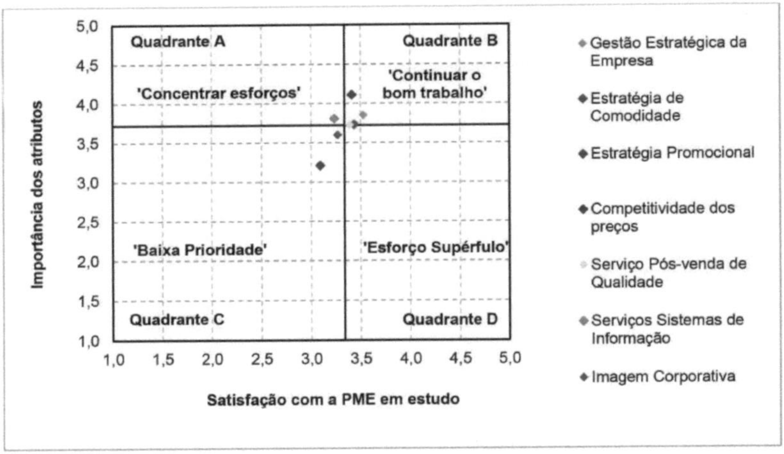

Figura 10 - Analysis of the quadrants for the FCS, with the axis on the averages (3.34;3.72).

Once again, it is essential to carry out a quadrant analysis based on the global median values, which are shown in Figure 11 where the axis is defined by the global median values (3.26;3.73) and for the FCS the global averages.

The company shows good results for Price competitiveness and Strategic management (Figure 11).

Efforts should be concentrated on the Information Systems Service FCS, the promotional strategy is in quadrant C, which represents a low priority, and corporate image is in quadrant D.

It is worth noting that the Quality After-Sales Services and Convenience Strategy are on the axis between quadrant B and D.

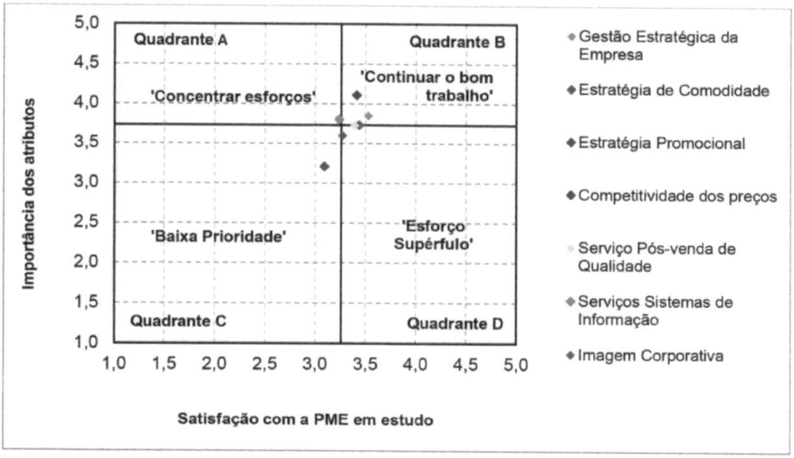

Figura 11 - Analysis of the quadrants for the FCS, with the axis at the medians (3.26;3.73).

3.3 - Exploratory Factor Analysis to Identify the KSFs that Maximize Customer Satisfaction at Futurlab

The aim here is to identify the Critical Success Factors (CSFs) for the Futurlab company, from the point of view of its customers. In other words, the main objective of this empirical study will be answered. To this end, Exploratory Factor Analysis will be applied to help recognize those CSFs that maximize customer satisfaction.

Therefore, in order to apply Exploratory Factor Analysis, it is necessary to verify its applicability by analyzing the *Kaiser-Meyer-Olkin* (KMO) measure and Bartlett's test of sphericity.

Analyzing the KMO value for the latent variable Importance, we see that the value is less than 0.5, making it unacceptable to proceed with Exploratory Factor Analysis. However, the significance value obtained for Bartlett's test of sphericity is less than 5% (significance level), so there is sufficient statistical evidence to state that the variables are not independent, i.e. they are correlated.

Since the KMO did not show satisfactory results, it was decided not to proceed with the Exploratory Factor Analysis for the latent variable Importance.

The same analysis was repeated for the latent variable Satisfaction and the KMO value was found to be 0.519. As there is a value above 0.5, it is considered acceptable to apply Exploratory Factor Analysis, as the value presented is not satisfactory, but it is still considered acceptable. By analyzing Bartlett's test of sphericity and since it shows a test value of less than 0.001, it can be inferred that there is sufficient statistical evidence to state that the variables are not independent, i.e. they are correlated, assuming a significance level of 5%.

It should be noted that the aim of this analysis is to identify the Critical Success Factors for the Futurlab company that maximize customer satisfaction, so it is considered correct and acceptable to work only with the latent variable Satisfaction to profile these CSFs from the customers' point of view.

In the analysis of all the assumptions for the application of Exploratory Factor Analysis, it was found through the analysis of the sample adequacy measure and the analysis of communalities that there was no need to remove variables from the questionnaire, as they all had values with a weight greater than 0.5.

The principal components method was chosen to extract the factors. In order to identify the number of factors, *Pearson*'s criterion was used, resulting in 7 factors with an accumulated variance percentage of 75.45% of the total variance.

In order to facilitate interpretation, the factors were rotated using the *Varimax* method, with the aim of extremizing the values of the weights so that each variable is associated with only one factor.

Table 17 shows the results of the Exploratory Factor Analysis, where the Critical Success Factors identified for Futurlab can be seen, thus answering the main objective of this empirical study.

Factor 1 explains 29.029% of the structure of the data. It is the most important factor in explaining the data under analysis. The other factors are relatively less important in summarizing the original variables. Factor 2 explains 13.857% of the variability in the data; factor 3 accounts for 7.796% of the explanation; factor 4 explains 7.601%; factor 5 is responsible for around 6.577% of the explanation; factor 6 explains 5.671% and finally factor 7, which explains 4.922% of the total variance.

Cronbach's Alpha coefficient was used to measure the reliability of the grouping of variables for each factor. It can be seen from the values in the following table that the factors have levels of internal consistency between Reasonable (factors 3, 5, 6 and 7) and Good for factors 1, 2 and 4 (Hill & Hill, 2009).

Table 15 - Critical Success Factors identified for the Futurlab Company

FCS/Satisfaction Items	Weights	% Variance	Own values	*Cronbach's alpha*	Commonalities

			Explained			
Factor 1 - Pricing Strategy and Free Services			**29,029**	**8,709**	**0,899**	
EP	Intense promotional or discount activities	0,726				,710
CP	Cheaper and more competitive products	0,637				,580
CP	Cheap maintenance and accessories	0,749				,785
SQ	Free maintenance services	0,831				,847
SQ	Installation services at the client company's premises	0,622				,785
SI	*Online* services such as product presentation and price research	0,823				,782
SI	Easy-to-use and convenient *online* services	0,803				,865
Factor 2 - Loyalty			**13,857**	**4,157**	**0,847**	
EC	Unique amenities	0,59				,607
EC	Having an organized and well-presented product display and distribution	0,495				,502
EP	Promotional activities for occasional congresses/seminars	0,692				,532
EP	A membership card system with low or very low membership fees	0,847				,770
CP	Money-back guarantee if found cheaper	0,571				,723
SQ	Free 24-hour telephone service	0,787				,855
SQ	Maintenance products for the home delivery service	0,763				,829
Factor 3 - Image			**7,796**	**2,339**	**0,786**	
GE	Suitable warehouse/store close to customer areas	0,669				,801
IC	Healthy financial position	0,765				,763
IC	Social activities within the community	0,774				,808
IC	Clarifying the company's mission	0,836				,844
Factor 4 - Supply and Stock			**7,601**	**2,28**	**0,823**	
GE	Adequate supply of products	0,605				,764
EC	Having a variety of products in stock.	0,798				,740
EC	Rapid substitution of products and placing new products on the market	0,777				,824
CP	Easy to interpret quotes with all the information you need	0,676				,682
Factor 5 - Information			**6,577**	**1,973**	**0,773**	
SQ	Easy access to information on the activities of the supplier/distributor company	0,631				,789
SI	*Online* professional advice	0,797				,790
SI	Suggestions and customer information calls	0,81				,809

Factor 6 - Logistics			**5,671**	**1,701**	**0,719**	
GE	Accurate and efficient distribution logistics	0,804				,763
SQ	Delivery services to the customer's premises	0,653				,653
IC	A reputable and credible company	0,713				,803
Factor 7 - Virtual Channels			**4,922**	**1,477**	**0,711**	
GE	Development of a virtual distribution channel	0,85				,818
EP	Creative promotional strategies for integration of both virtual and practical channels	0,652				,813

It is possible to attribute explanatory facts to behaviors, given the nature of the variables that most explain each of the factors.

So, in order to explain the contribution of the variables to each of the Critical Success Factors identified, and based on the table above, the factors found were categorized according to the attributes that explain them:

- Factor 1: variables related to promotional strategies, price competitiveness, quality after-sales services and information systems services, which we have called **Price Strategy and Free Services**;
- Factor 2: includes Convenience Strategy, Promotional Strategy, Price Competitiveness and Quality After-Sales Service. This factor was therefore identified as **Loyalty**;
- Factor 3 groups together the variables related to Strategic Management and Corporate **Image**;
- Factor 4: associates Strategic Management with Strategic Convenience and Price Competitiveness. This factor is called **Supply and Stock**;
- Factor 5: groups together the variables related to quality after-sales services and systems and information services. This factor has therefore been given the name **Information**;
- Factor 6: The variables related to strategic management, quality after-sales services and corporate image are brought together in the sixth factor. It has been called **Logistics**;
- Factor 7: the variables related to Strategic Management and Promotional Strategy are grouped together and given the name **Virtual Channels**.

For a better understanding of the grouping made, the following table summarizes the different factors with the different attributes that make up each Critical Success Factor identified for Futurlab.

Table 16 - Summary of the attributes that explain the KSFs identified for Futurlab.

Factor	**Attributes**	**Critical Success Factors**
Factor 1	Intense promotional or discount activities Cheaper and more competitive products Cheap maintenance and accessories Free maintenance services Installation services at the client company's premises Providing *online* services such as product displays and price searches Easy-to-use and convenient *online* services	*Pricing Strategy and Grâtis Services*
Factor 2	Unique amenities Having an organized and well-presented display and distribution of products Promotional activities for occasional congresses/seminars A membership card system with free or low-yield memberships Money-back guarantee if found cheaper Free 24-hour telephone service Maintenance products for the home delivery service	*Loyalty*
Factor 3	Suitable warehouse/store close to customer areas Healthy financial position Social activities within the community Clarifying the company's mission	*Image*
Factor 4	Adequate supply of products Having a variety of products in stock. Rapid substitution of products and placing new products on the market Easy to interpret quotes with all the information you need	*Supply and Stock*
Factor 5	Easy access to information on the activities of the supplier/distributor company *Online* professional advice Suggestions and customer information calls	*Information*
	Accurate and efficient distribution logistics	

Factor 6	Delivery services to the customer's premises A reputable and credible company	*Logistics*
Factor 7	Development of a virtual distribution channel Creative promotional strategies for integrating both virtual and practical channels	*Virtual Channels*

3.4 - Validation of the Research Hypotheses

As already mentioned, one of the more specific objectives of this work was to find out whether the KSFs identified in the previous point maximize customer satisfaction at Futurlab, and so the following research hypotheses were established:

Research Hypothesis 1: Futurlab's customers are satisfied with all the identified KSFs;

Research Hypothesis 2: There is a positive relationship between the KSFs and overall satisfaction with Futurlab.

The aim here is to statistically corroborate the hypotheses raised.

The following table shows the total values for each of the KSFs that maximize customer satisfaction at Futurlab. The values presented show that the maximum values obtained in the empirical study are very close to the theoretical maximum values, which is a very satisfactory result for the company. Also, when comparing the values between the theoretical average and the empirical average obtained, it can be seen that the latter was 10.3022 points above the theoretical average, which is very satisfactory for the company.

The values recorded for the standard deviation for each KSF were also low, making it possible to note that there was almost no variability between the answers given by the respondents.

Thus, customers are very satisfied with the following KSFs: Pricing Strategies and Free Services, Loyalty and Image. The factors offering the least satisfaction were Virtual Channels and Logistics.

Table 17 - Statistical summary for each FCS that maximizes customer satisfaction at Futurlab.

FCS for Futurlab	Minimum	Maximo	Maximo Possible	Average Theoretical	Average Empirical	Deviation Standard	*Z-Score*	*Ranking*
Pricing Strategy and Free Services	12,00	35,00	35	21	23,5556	5,21312	0,490216	1
Loyalty	12,00	31,00	35	21	21,3422	3,70247	0,092431	2

Image	10,00	20,00	20	12	15,0978	2,58071	1,2003613
Supply and Stock	5,00	17,00	20	12	12,6622	2,05974	0,3215074
Information	7,00	14,00	15	9	11,6756	1,78950	1,4951435
Logistics	5,00	14,00	15	9	9,4933	1,95055	0,25292 6
Virtual Channels	4,00	9,00	10	6	6,4756	1,23584	0,3848037
Total score	66,00	125,00	150	90	100,3022	12,48561	0,825128-

Furthermore, based on the theoretical average of 90 points and applying the *Student's t-test, we* obtained a test value of 12.377 (224 degrees of freedom) and a test value of less than 0.001, so we can say that Research Hypothesis 1 has been corroborated, as there is sufficient statistical evidence to affirm that the average is significantly different from 90 points, assuming a significance level of 5%.

The following table shows the *Likert* scale used in the questionnaire applied to an overall variable resulting from the composition of the 30 variables in relation to Overall Satisfaction with the services provided by Futurlab. The aim of this analysis is to verify an overall evaluation of responses that tend to be negative or positive. It can be seen from the analysis that the majority of responses are in the Satisfied and Very Satisfied categories, 27.4% and 10.2% respectively, overall 37.6% against 11.7% Dissatisfied. However, there is a percentage of responses that fall into the Indifference category (50.7%). This behavior can also be seen when analyzing the percentage of responses over the number of respondents.

Table 18 - Overall satisfaction assessment.

Likert scale	Answers		% of respondents
	n	%	
Very Dissatisfied	117	1,7	52,0
Dissatisfied	673	10,0	299,1
Neither dissatisfied nor satisfied	3423	50,7	1521,3
Satisfied	1849	27,4	821,8
Very satisfied	688	10,2	305,8
Total	**6750**	**100,0**	**3000,0**

Moving on to the positioning of the KSFs identified for Futurlab in the Quadrant Analysis, using the Importance *vs.* Satisfaction Matrix (Figure 12), it can be seen that the factors were distributed in 2 quadrants (quadrant B and quadrant C).

In quadrant B were the KSFs Logistics, Supply and Stock and Price strategy and free services. These were highly important and satisfactory in the perception of Futurlab's customers, so they are KSFs that represent opportunities to gain or maintain competitive advantages in the market where Futurlab operates. These Factors are extremely important to customers and perform well, so Futurlab should continue the good work reflected in the attributes that make up these Factors.

Quadrant C, represented by low importance and satisfaction, included the KSFs Information, Virtual channels, Image and Loyalty; therefore, as they are low priority, there is no need to concentrate efforts.

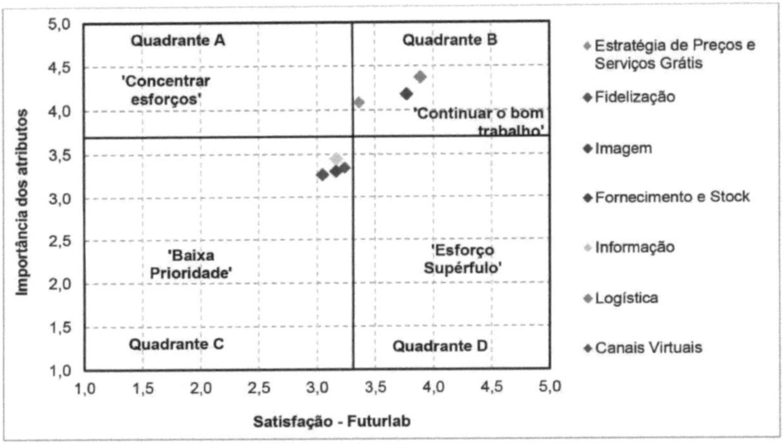

Figura 12 - Analysis of the quadrants for the FCS averages, with the axis at the medians (3.26;3.73).

According to the figures presented and in the opinion of the authors of this research, Futurlab's managers should prioritize and intervene in the attributes that make up the factors positioned in quadrant C, since these KSFs have an explained variance of 33.152%.

It should be noted that in the previous Importance *vs.* Satisfaction Analysis, using the KSFs from the study by Wu, Tang and Shyu (2009), it was concluded that the Promotional Strategy was a point of low satisfaction and importance, a fact that is now proven in these factors made up of promotional strategy variables.

In order to answer the second research hypothesis, an intensity analysis was carried out between Futurlab's KSFs and Global Satisfaction, i.e. the aim was to describe the magnitude and direction between the KSFs and the latent variable Global Satisfaction. *Pearson*'s correlation coefficient was used as there was no violation of the normality assumption (Table 20).

When analyzing the correlations between the Factors and the total score, it can be said that all the Factors are correlated with Global Satisfaction, at a significance level of 1%. In other words, they have a direct positive relationship both with Global Satisfaction and with each other, which validates the second research hypothesis.

Thus, the KSFs that showed a high correlation coefficient with Overall Satisfaction were: Factor 1 - Pricing Strategy and Free Services (0.803); Factor 2 - Loyalty (0.704) and Factor 4 - Supply and Stock (0.701). In other words, they have a strong, positive, direct and statistically significant relationship with Overall Satisfaction. On the other hand, although statistically significant, there is Factor 5 - Information, where the relationship with Overall Satisfaction is weaker, but positive and direct.

Among the KSFs, the most correlated are: Factor 1 - Pricing Strategy and Free Services with Factor 6 - Logistics, with a correlation coefficient of 0.537, and with Factor 4 - Supply and Stock (0.532); which means that there is a direct and positive relationship between these 3 Factors and designates the force that holds them together. Factor 5 - Information is the one with the lowest correlation with factor 3 - Image.

Table 19 - *Pearson* correlation between Futurlab's KSFs and overall satisfaction.

	F1	F2	F3	F4	F5	F6	F7	**Overall satisfaction**
Pricing Strategy and Free Services	1	,300	,319	,532	,198	,537	,264	**,803**
Loyalty		1	,413	,312	,461	,255	,412	**,704**
Image			1	,289	,141	,159	,260	**,551**
Supply and Stock				1	,240	,461	,284	**,701**
Information					1	,175	,319	**,505**
Logistics						1	,308	**,623**
Virtual Channels							1	**,527**
Overall satisfaction								**1**

After all the analysis presented and explained above, it can be said that the main objectives of this research have been met, as well as the corroboration of the research hypotheses.

3.5 - *CLUSTER* ANALYSIS

In order to complement this empirical study and to identify homogeneous groups of customers who give importance to Futurlab's KSFs, we decided to carry out a classificatory analysis, namely *Cluster* Analysis, which divides the initial set of cases - Futurlab's customers - into several subsets - the *clusters*.

Hierarchical *cluster* analysis was applied using the Euclidean distance between the cases and the *Complete Linkage* method. In this method, once the first *cluster has been* formed, its distance from the other cases is the greatest of the distances of each of the elements making up this cluster from each of the other cases (Marôco, 2010).

To define the optimum number of *clusters* to retain, the *r* criterion was used, with the help of *One-Way ANOVA,* as well as the graph of the distance between *clusters* relativized and r2. The *r-criterion "is* a measure of the total variability that is retained in each of the *cluster* solutions" (Marôco, 2010, p. 567).

We worked out a solution of between 2 and 8 *clusters*, so after applying the criteria mentioned above, we opted for an optimum solution of four *clusters*, which explains around 39% of the total variability. To help validate this information, we used a graphical representation of the distance between *clusters* relativized and the coefficient of determination (Figure 13), concluding that the optimum number of *clusters* is 4.

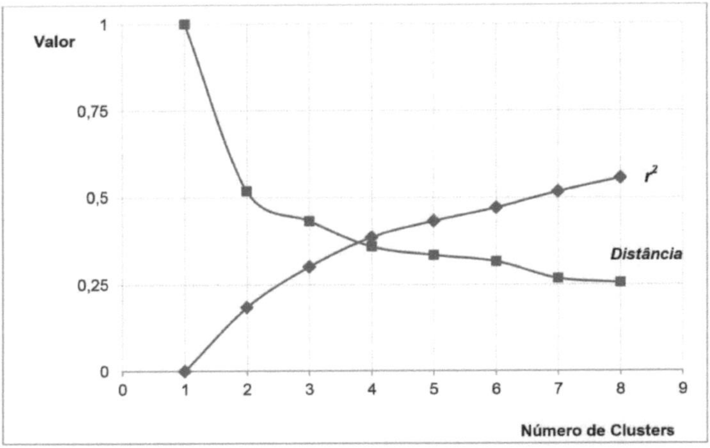

Figura 13 - Optimal number of *clusters*.

Based on the grouping made, the number of companies that fall into each *cluster was* extracted and shown in the following table.

Table 20 - Number of Futurlab customers, by *cluster*.

Cluster 1	49 customers
Cluster 2	94 customers
Cluster 3	69 customers
Cluster 4	13 customers

After an exhaustive analysis of the distribution of the different customers among the homogeneous groups identified, based on each of the attributes of the latent variable Importance under study, as well as the Critical Success Factors identified, it was possible to classify each *cluster* extracted. In order to classify them, each of the CSFs was taken into account, and when it was assigned to a *cluster*, it could not be repeated in subsequent analyses.

In this context, the results obtained are presented below:

- **Analysis of *Cluster 1* - Importance for Information and Loyalty**

This *cluster* is made up of 49 clients, 17 of whom are male and 32 female, most of whom are between 26 and 35 years old, and most of whom have Bachelor's and Master's degrees. These clients are laboratory technicians and research fellows. The companies are teaching and/or research companies and external laboratories, located in the Central and Lisbon/Tejo areas.

- ***Cluster* 2 Analysis - Importance for Image**

This *cluster* is made up of 94 clients. Of the managers who responded to the questionnaire, 34 are male and 60 are female, the majority are aged between 31 and 50, and the majority are Bachelors, Masters and Doctors. The clients are laboratory technicians, purchasing technicians and laboratory managers. The companies are food, pharmaceutical and education and/or research industries, located in the Central and Lisbon/Tejo areas and Porto and the North.

- **Analysis of *Cluster* 3 - Importance for Supply and Stock and for Virtual Channels**

This *cluster* is made up of 69 clients, 33 of whom are male and 36 female, most of whom are between 31 and 50 years old, and most of whom have Bachelor's, Master's or PhD degrees. They are laboratory technicians, teachers and purchasing technicians. The companies are external laboratories and teaching and/or research facilities, located in the

Lisbon/Tejo area and Porto and the North.

◦ **Analysis of *Cluster* 4 - Importance for Pricing Strategy and Services Grâtis Logistica**

This *cluster* is made up of 13 clients. Of these, 4 are male and 9 are female, most are between 26 and 55 years old, and most have a Master's degree. These are individuals who are research fellows and professors. The companies are teaching and/or research companies located in the Lisbon/Tejo area.

In order to analyze the importance that each *cluster* attributed to the Critical Success Factors identified for Futurlab, the following figure was produced. The average of the scores obtained for each CSF was calculated based on the Importance dimension, by *cluster*.

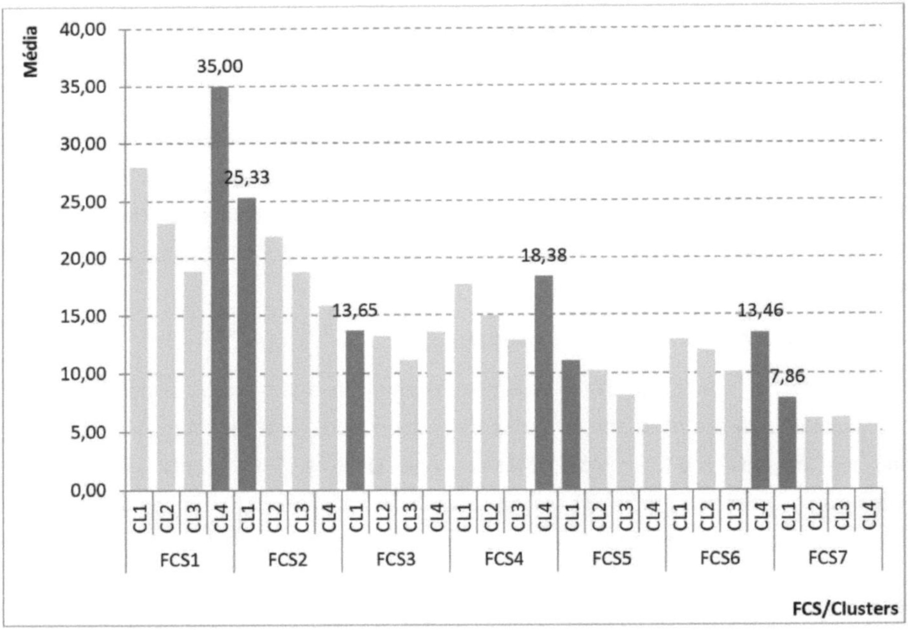

Note: CL1 - Cluster 1; CL2 - Cluster 2; CL3 - Cluster 3; CL4 - Cluster 4. FCS1 - Pricing Strategy and Free Services; FCS2 - Loyalty; FCS3 - Image; FCS4 - Supply and Stock; FCS5 - Information; FCS6 - Logistics; FCS7 - Virtual Channels.

Figure 14 - Summary of cluster averages for each of Futurlab's FCS.

From the analysis of the values and information reflected in the figure above and based on the degree of importance attributed to each KSF, the following can be concluded:

- For KSF 1 - Pricing Strategy and Free Services, *cluster* 4 was the group that had the highest average, leading us to consider that it attributed capital importance to this factor;
- For KSF 2 - Loyalty, it was *cluster* 1 that attached particular importance;
- For KSF 3 - Image, *cluster* 1 recorded the highest average importance of the *clusters*, followed by *cluster* 4 and *Cluster* 2;
- For KSF 4 - Supply and Stock, *cluster* 4 had the highest average importance, followed by *cluster* 1 and *cluster* 2 in third place;
- For KSF 5 - Information, the *clusters with the* highest averages were *cluster* 1, followed by *clusters* 2 and 3;
- For KSF 6 - Logistics, *cluster* 4 had the highest average importance, followed by *clusters* 1 and 2;
- For KSF 7 - Virtual Channels, the *clusters with the* highest averages were *cluster* 1, followed by *clusters* 3 and 2.

From this analysis it can be concluded that the KSFs Pricing Strategy and Free Services, Loyalty, Supply and Stock, and Image are the ones that companies attach particular importance to; as already mentioned in previous analyses. On the other hand, the KSFs with the lowest averages in terms of importance were Information, Logistics and Virtual Channels.

It should also be noted that *Clusters* 1 and 4 have the highest values for each of the KSFs. Based on these values, it can be said that this group of laboratory technicians and research fellows will be more demanding of the services provided.

4. CONCLUSION AND FUTURE LINES OF RESEARCH

The aim of this study was to identify Critical Success Factors in the development of strategies to maximize customer satisfaction at Futurlab - Material de Laboratório Lda, based in Lisbon.

The aim of this work was to analyze the satisfaction and importance attributed by the company's customers, to identify the dimensions related to the quality of the services provided that influence satisfaction and, of course, to visualize the company's ability to attract and retain its customers.

To this end, the sample consisted of 225 clients who were managers of the companies they represented, corresponding to 21% of the population, of which 39% were male and 61% female. The age of the clients surveyed ranged from 19 to over 56, and 53.3% were university graduates. The majority (58.2%) of the companies were based in the Lisbon and Tagus area, of which 23.6% were educational/research companies.

From the research carried out and analyzing the Importance *vs.* Satisfaction matrix with the total initial variables of the questionnaire survey proposed to customers, it was found that efforts need to be concentrated on improving free maintenance services, this is an attribute of high importance and where dissatisfaction is evident. Futurlab should focus on reformulating creative promotional strategies to integrate virtual channels such as praticals. This is a superfluous effort for the company and is of low importance despite customer satisfaction.

This theory was proven by analyzing the initial latent variables into which the questionnaire survey proposed to customers was divided, concluding that there are good results for price competitiveness and strategic management, and that improvements are recommended in terms of quality after-sales services. Special care should be taken and efforts concentrated on the Information Systems Service attribute. It is advisable to reformulate promotional strategies, and corporate image is considered to be an unnecessary effort.

In order to assess which dimensions are most used by customers, both in evaluating the importance of certain attributes that a company in the sector should have and in evaluating the quality of the services provided by Futurlab, we identified the Critical Success Factors using Exploratory Factor Analysis and then analyzed the degree of satisfaction of Futurlab's customers, applying the Matrix of Importance vs. Satisfaction to the Critical Success Factors identified. As a result, it was found that the good work on the Pricing and Free Services, Supply and Stock and Logistics strategies should be maintained and that the Loyalty, Image, Information and Virtual Channels strategies should be reformulated, as they are not considered important factors, and Futurlab should therefore redefine these factors in order to make them important and improve customer satisfaction.

The *Cluster* Analysis identified 4 *Clusters* according to the importance attributed to the Critical Success Factors, namely: *Cluster* 1 - Importance of Information and Loyalty; *Cluster* 2 - Importance of Image; *Cluster* 3 - Importance of Supply and Stock and Virtual Channels; *Cluster* 4 - Importance of Pricing Strategy and Grâtis Logistica Services.

In general, customers are satisfied with Futurlab's performance and Futurlab has all the necessary conditions to offer quality services in order to attract new customers and retain its current ones. Satisfied customers contribute to their loyalty to the company by staying with the company for future purchases.

To finish off this analysis, we wanted to see if there were any differences between female and male customers in terms of Overall Satisfaction and Overall Importance, by age group, educational level, position held in the company, type of company, net profit, frequency of visits and company location. Using parametric and non-parametric tests, it was concluded that there is sufficient statistical evidence to affirm that at least one of the distributions for Overall Satisfaction in the age and position groups is different, and the same is true for Overall Importance. The type of company or sector of activity and the company location variable have a different effect on Overall Satisfaction. For the variables company location, educational qualifications, net profit, frequency of visits and gender, there are no statistically significant differences in the responses in relation to Overall Satisfaction and Overall Importance.

Thus, the analysis carried out corroborates the research hypotheses. In other words, customers are globally satisfied with the Critical Success Factors identified for Futurlab and the correlations between the Factors and the total score show a direct positive relationship both with Global Satisfaction and between them, assuming a significance level of 5%.

This research makes an important contribution because it has made it possible to identify the level of customer satisfaction at Futurlab, which has never been analyzed before. It has also made it possible to identify the attributes and dimensions related to the quality of the services provided that influence customer satisfaction and to visualize the company's ability to attract, keep and retain its customers.

In this way, this research also helped to identify the Critical Success Factors that need to be addressed by Futurlab's managers and to emphasize that they should prioritize and intervene in Loyalty, Image, Information and Virtual Channels. According to the authors of this research, image is very important for the company, since appearance is the first contact customers have with the company, so it is essential that the sales network and the company's corporate image exceed customer expectations in order to retain customers and win new ones. This service therefore requires intervention by Futurlab's management.

As with any study, this one was not without its limitations, as its results may be somewhat biased due to the length of the questionnaire, 30 variables for Importance plus 30 variables for Satisfaction, causing a repetitive effect in the answers. It is believed that this was not the case, as the values presented for internal consistency recorded by *Cronbach's Alpha* were high. Even so, the questionnaire was applied in the context of the crisis that is plaguing Portugal, so customer sentiment and behavior may be reflected in a more negative attitude towards the company under study.

Future lines of research are presented below:

- to monitor the Critical Success Factors identified, as well as to apply the questionnaire in a more favorable context for Futurlab's surroundings, as we want the business to flourish and the company's objectives to be achieved;
- Since the company feels the need to provide a quality service that will enable it to attract and retain customers, raising awareness of quality among companies in the same line of business entails the need to evaluate it, which presupposes the adoption of measuring instruments;
- In order to validate the *cluster* analysis, it would be interesting to carry out a *path* analysis in order to understand the relationship between the latent variables and the Critical Success Factors identified. This analysis has already been carried out by the authors of this study, but despite presenting satisfactory values in various evaluation parameters, the analysis was accepted but the model needed to be improved.

Finally, it can be concluded that there are many opportunities for future research in this field, as it is a very broad area of investigation.

5. BIBLIOGRAPHICAL REFERENCES

Abalo, J., Varela, J., & Manzano, V. (2007). Importance values for Importance-Performance Analysis: A formula for spreading out values derived from preference rankings. *Journal of Business Research*, 60(2), 115-121.

Aktas, A., Aksu, A., & Çizel, B. (2007). Destination choice: An Important - Satisfaction Analysis. *Quality & Quality*, 41, 265-273.

Atamer, T., & Calori, R. (1993). *Diagnostic and strategic decisions.* 1ª edition, Paris: Dunod.

Bailey, S. (1987). *Using the Critical Success Factor Method to Develop a Strategic Managerial Action Plan.* Master's Thesis, M.I.T., Massachusetts Institute of Technology, Sloan School of Management.

Baranano, A. (2004). Research Methods and Techniques in Management. 1ª Edition, Lisbon: Ediçôes Silabo.

Baxter, J. (1983). Managers: What's Critical to Your Success*?, Iron Age*, 226 (5), 37-39.

Bouquin, H. (1986). *Management control.* 1ª edition. Paris: Presses Universitaires de France.

Boynton, A., & Zmud, R. (1984). An assessment of critical success factors. *Management Review*, 25 (4), 17-27.

Caralli, R. (2004). *The Critical Success Factor Method: Establishing a Foundation for Enterprise Security Management.* Software Engineering Institute, Carnegie Mellon, Pittsburgh

Churchill, G. (1979). A paradigm for developing better measures of marketing constructs. *Journal of Marketing Research*, 16 (1), 64-73.

Costa, B. (2008). Quality Management Systems in Portuguese Companies: Implementation, Impact and Performance. Doctoral Thesis. University of Seville.

Crato, C. (2010). *Quality: Condition for Competitiveness.* Porto, SPI - Sociedade Portuguesa de Inovaçâo Consultadoria Empresarial e Fomento da Inovaçâo.

Drucker, P. (1967) *The Effective Executive.* New York: E.P. Dutton.

Forster, N., & Rockart, J. (1989). *Critical Success Factors: An Annotated Bibliography.* Working Paper No. 191. Center for Information Systems Research, Sloan School of Management Massachusetts Institute of Technology.

Freire, A. (2008). Strategy - Success in Portugal. 12ª edition, Lisbon: Verbo.

Garrette, B. (1993). *Stratégie, structure, décision, identité: politique générale d'entreprise*. 2ª edition, Paris: Interedition.

Gomes, P. (2004). *The Evolution of the Concept of Quality: from Manufactured Goods to Information Services*, Cadernos BAD 2, 6-18.

Hill, M., & Hill, A. (2009). *Investigaçâo por Questionàrio*. 2ª edition. Lisbon: Ediçôes Silabo.

Hofer, C., & Schendel, D. (1978). *Strategy Formulation: Analytical Concepts (The West Series in Business Policy and planning.* West Publishing Company.

Koenig G, (1990). *Management Stratégique: Vision, manoeuvres et tactiques*. Paris: Nathan.

Leidecker, J., & Bruno, A. (1984). Identifying and using critical success factors. *Long Range Planning*, 17, 23-32.

Lynch, J., Carver, R., & Virgo, J. (1996). Quadrant analysis as a strategic planning technique in curriculum development and program marketing. *Journal of Marketing for Higher Education*, 7 (2), 17-32.

Magretta, J. (2012). *Michael Porter. The essentials of Strategy, Competition and Competitiveness*. Atlantic Center. Portugal

Marôco, J. (2010). Statistical Analysis with PASW Statistics (formerly SPSS). 5th edition. Pêro Pinheiro: Report Numbers.

Martilla, J., & James, J. (1977). Importance-Performance Analysis. *Journal of Marketing*, 77-79.

Matzler, K., Sauerwein, E., & Heischmidt, K. (2003). Importance-performance analysis Revisited: the role of the factor structure of customer satisfaction. *The Service Industries Journal*, 23 (2), 112-129.

Neves, J. (2003). *Managing organizational culture: from content to process*. In Lima, L., Castro, P.; & Garrido, M. (eds), Temas e debates em psicologia social. Lisbon: Livros Horizonte.

Oliveira, O. (2006). *Quality Management: Advanced Topics*. Sâo Paulo Pioneira Thomson Learning, Sâo Paulo.

Paladini, E. (2000). *Quality management: theory and practice*. Atlas: Sâo Paulo.

Porter, M. (1986). *Competitive Strategy: Techniques for Analyzing Industries and*

Competition (7th Edition). Rio de Janeiro: Campus.

Porter, M. (1996). What is Strategy. *Harvard Business Review,* 96608, 59-78.

Quintella, H., Rocha, H., & Alves, M. (2005). Automotive vehicle projects: critical success factors at launch. *Revista Produçao*, 15 (3), 334-346.

Ribeiro, A. (2009). *Concepts and Principles of Quality*. Master's dissertation. School of Technology, Polytechnic Institute of Càvado and Ave.

Rigopoulou, I., Chaniotakis, I., Lymperopoulos, C., & Siomkos, G. (2008). After-sales service quality as an antecedent of customer satisfaction: The case of electronic appliances. *Managing Service Quality*, 18 (5), 512-527.

Rockart, J. (1979). Chief Executives Define Their Own Data Needs. *Harvard Business Review*, 57, 81-83.

Silva, F., & Fernandes, P. (2010). *Using Importance-Performance Analysis in Evaluating of Higher Education: A Case Study*. ICEMT 2010 International Conference on Education and Management Technology. IEEE. 121-123.

Skogland, I., & Siguaw, J. (2004). Are Your Satisfied Customers Loyal? Cornell Hospitality Quarterly, 45 (3), 221-234.

Verstraete, T. (2000). *Essai de Conceptualisation de la Notion de Facteur Clé de Succès et de Facteur Stratégique de Risque*. CLAEĖE - Centre Lillois d'Analyse et de Recherche sur l'Evolution des Entreprises, URA. CNRS 936.

Waal, A., & Gerritsen-Medema, G. (2006). Performance management analysis: a case study at a Dutch municipality - Maastricht School of Management, Netherlands. *International Journal of Productivity and Performance Management*, 55 (1), 26-39.

Wu, H., Tang, T., Shyu, W. (2009) A case of applying importance-performance analysis in identifying key success factors to develop marketing strategies. *Quality & Quantity*, 44 (6), 1207-1218.

ANNEX I - REQUEST FOR PERMISSION TO ADMINISTER QUESTIONNAIRES AND RESPECTIVE AUTHORIZATION

Dear Sir^{a} Managing Partner of FuturlabLda

As a student on the Master's Degree in Organizational Management - Business Management Branch - at the Polytechnic Institute of Bragança, within the framework of APNOR, I am writing to you to request permission to carry out a survey of Futurlab's customers.

The dissertation is on the subject of "identifying critical success factors in the development of strategies that maximize customer satisfaction". The aim is to study the degree of importance in the development of critical marketing factors and to associate customer satisfaction with the strategies adopted by the company, thus studying Futurlab's performance. In view of the aim of the study, it is necessary to obtain individual statistical information on the target population. This information can only be obtained through direct customer surveys.

The questionnaire I intend to use is anonymous and voluntary, with no identification or link between the respondent and the data collected.

I would like to thank you in advance for your attention to my request and make the results and conclusions of my research available to the company. I also remain at the company's disposal for any further clarification.

Best regards,

Bragança, March 14th, 2011

Helder Pires Ferreira

ANNEX II - DECLARATION OF THE COMPANY'S ACCEPTANCE OF THIS STUDY AND THE VERACITY OF THE STUDY APPLIED TO CUSTOMERS

DECLARATION

The company FUTURLAB - Material de Laboratòrio declares for all intents and purposes that Helder Pires Ferreira, a former salesman for this company, is carrying out a research project as part of his Master's Degree in Organizational Management at the School of Technology and Management (ESTIG) of the Polytechnic Institute of Bragança (IPB), with the aim of analyzing the degree of customer satisfaction with the services provided by Futurlab.

Therefore, in view of the need to gather opinions on the level of satisfaction with the services provided by FUTURLAB, we would like to ask for your cooperation in filling in the questionnaire that has been sent to you.

Without further ado, thank you in advance for your cooperation.

FUTURLAB
Material de Laboratório, Lda.
A Gerência

ANNEX III - QUESTIONNAIRE

NORTHERN POLYTECHNIC ASSOCIATION **(APNOR)**

BRAGANÇA POLYTECHNIC INSTITUTE

MASTER'S IN ORGANIZATIONAL MANAGEMENT

BUSINESS MANAGEMENT

I'm a student on the Master's course in Organizational Management at the School of Technology and Management (ESTIG) of the Polytechnic Institute of Bragança (IPB), run by the Association of Polytechnics of the North (APNOR).

As part of my Master's thesis, I am carrying out a piece of research which aims to analyze the level of customer satisfaction with the services provided by Futurlab. Therefore, in view of the need to collect opinions on the level of satisfaction with the services provided by the company mentioned above, I would ask for your cooperation in completing this questionnaire.

Responses will be anonymous and confidential, so please do not provide any information other than that requested in order to maintain anonymity and confidentiality.

THANK YOU VERY MUCH FOR YOUR COLLABORATION.

I. "**Analysis of the importance of developing marketing strategies for Futurlab**"

In order to analyze the importance you attach to the services provided by Futurlab, please answer the following questions by circling your choice on the following scale:

1=Not Important; **2=Little Important**; **3=Relatively Important**; **4=Very Important**; 5=Extremely Important

MANAGEMENT COMPANY STRATEGY						
1	Suitable warehouse/store near customer premises	1	2	3	4	5
2	Adequate supply of products	1	2	3	4	5
3	Accurate and efficient distribution logistics	1	2	3	4	5
4	Development of a virtual distribution channel	1	2	3	4	5
CONVENIENCE STRATEGY						
5	Having a variety of products in stock.	1	2	3	4	5
6	Rapid substitution of products and placing new products on the market	1	2	3	4	5
7	Unique amenities	1	2	3	4	5
8	Having an organized and well-presented display and distribution of products	1	2	3	4	5
PROMOTIONAL STRATEGY						
9	Creative promotional strategies for integrating both virtual and practical channels	1	2	3	4	5
10	Promotional activities for occasional congresses/seminars	1	2	3	4	5
11	Intense promotional or discount activities	1	2	3	4	5
12	A membership card system with free or low-yield memberships	1	2	3	4	5
PRICE COMPETITIVENESS						
13	Cheaper and more competitive products	1	2	3	4	5
14	Cheap maintenance and accessories	1	2	3	4	5
15	Easy to interpret quotes with all the information you need	1	2	3	4	5
16	Money-back guarantee if found cheaper	1	2	3	4	5
QUALITY AFTER-SALES SERVICES						
17	Free 24-hour telephone service	1	2	3	4	5
18	Free maintenance services	1	2	3	4	5
19	Delivery services to the customer's premises	1	2	3	4	5
20	Installation services at the client company's premises	1	2	3	4	5
21	Easy access to information on the activities of the supplier/distributor company	1	2	3	4	5
22	Maintenance products for the home delivery service	1	2	3	4	5
SERVICES INFORMATION SYSTEMS						
23	*Online* professional advice	1	2	3	4	5
24	Providing *online* services such as product displays and price searches	1	2	3	4	5
25	Easy-to-use and convenient *online* services	1	2	3	4	5
26	Calls for suggestions and customer information	1	2	3	4	5
CORPORATE IMAGE						
27	A reputable and credible company	1	2	3	4	5
28	Healthy financial position	1	2	3	4	5
29	Social activities within the community	1	2	3	4	5
30	Clarifying the company's mission	1	2	3	4	5

II. "Analysis of the level of satisfaction with the services provided by Futurlab"

In order to analyze your level of satisfaction with the services provided by Futurlab, please answer the following questions by circling your choice on the following scale:

1=Very Dissatisfied; **2=Dissatisfied**; **3=Neither Dissatisfied** nor Satisfied; **4=Satisfied**; **5=Very** Satisfied

COMPANY STRATEGY MANAGEMENT						
1	Suitable warehouse/store close to customer areas	1	2	3	4	5
2	Adequate supply of products	1	2	3	4	5
3	Accurate and efficient distribution logistics	1	2	3	4	5
4	Development of a virtual distribution channel	1	2	3	4	5
CONVENIENCE STRATEGY						
5	Having a variety of products in stock	1	2	3	4	5
6	Rapid substitution of products and placing new products on the market	1	2	3	4	5
7	Unique amenities	1	2	3	4	5
8	Having an organized and well-presented display and distribution of products	1	2	3	4	5
PROMOTIONAL STRATEGY						
9	Creative promotional strategies for integrating both virtual and practical channels	1	2	3	4	5
10	Promotional activities for occasional congresses/seminars	1	2	3	4	5
11	Intense promotional or discount activities	1	2	3	4	5
12	A membership card system with low or very low membership fees	1	2	3	4	5
PRICE COMPETITIVENESS						
13	Cheaper and more competitive products	1	2	3	4	5
14	Cheap maintenance and accessories	1	2	3	4	5
15	Easy to interpret quotes with all the information you need	1	2	3	4	5
16	Money-back guarantee if found cheaper	1	2	3	4	5
QUALITY AFTER-SALES SERVICES						
17	Free 24-hour telephone service	1	2	3	4	5
18	Free maintenance services	1	2	3	4	5
19	Delivery services to the customer's premises	1	2	3	4	5
20	Installation services at the client company's premises	1	2	3	4	5
21	Easy access to information on the activities of the supplier/distributor company	1	2	3	4	5
22	Maintenance products for the home delivery service	1	2	3	4	5
SERVICES INFORMATION SYSTEMS						
23	*Online* professional advice	1	2	3	4	5
24	Providing *online* services such as product displays and price searches	1	2	3	4	5
25	Easy-to-use and convenient *online* services	1	2	3	4	5
26	Suggestions and customer information calls	1	2	3	4	5
CORPORATE IMAGE						
27	A reputable and credible company	1	2	3	4	5
28	Healthy financial position	1	2	3	4	5
29	Social activities within the community	1	2	3	4	5
30	Clarifying the company's mission	1	2	3	4	5

MIX
Papier aus verantwortungsvollen Quellen
Paper from responsible sources
FSC® C105338

Printed by Books on Demand GmbH, Norderstedt / Germany